A O Dyson

Who is Jesus Christ?

SCM PRESS LTD

334 01786 6

First published 1969
by SCM Press Ltd
56 Bloomsbury Street London WC1

© *SCM Press Ltd 1969*

Printed in Great Britain by
Billing & Sons Limited
Guildford and London

scm centrebooks

Christianity at the Centre / John Hick
Who is God? / D. W. D. Shaw
What about the Old Testament? / John Bowden
What is the New Testament? / T. G. A. Baker
What is the Church? / Victor de Waal
What is Right? / Michael Keeling
The Last Things Now / David L. Edwards
Who is Jesus Christ? / A. O. Dyson
What is Man? / David E. Jenkins

Contents

	Preface	7
1	The Great Breach in the Dam	9
2	The Critical Canons of Historical Thinking	29
3	Jesus Christ and the Demand of the 'Moment'	46
4	The Decisive Manifestation of Divine Love	63
5	Reading the Cipher of Jesus	76
6	Relating the Symbol of Christ to our Existence	94
7	Christ in the World of Matter	112
	Conclusion	123
	For Further Reading	125
	Index	126

Preface

A question can be defined both as the 'putting of a problem' and as the 'demand for an answer'. In this short book I am primarily occupied with the first of these definitions. *For my chief purpose is to examine some of the problems which are involved in framing the question 'Who is Jesus Christ?'* To illustrate this discussion I shall offer some preliminary descriptions and estimates of certain moments in the modern history of theological reflection.

I hold the view that there are many points of entry to the theme of Jesus Christ. Certainly I have no wish to devalue the currency of historical and biblical approaches which become essential when we seek to go beyond the preliminary questions which concern me here. None the less, the style of book which I have tried to write – in which I take samples of different points of view – closely reflects my own belief that theology is a complex and man-centred enterprise of analysis and interpretation which swings ceaselessly backwards and forwards between the understanding which we have of the world and the understanding of the world which the tradition about Jesus Christ proposes to us. I have therefore selected for consideration theological writers who to my mind represent this standpoint. The fact that all my chosen authors belong to the last hundred years is not intended as a slur on some eighteen centuries of previous reflection, but rather as an expression of my attempt to indicate that the structure of the theological enterprise has been truly called into question in recent times in such a way as profoundly to affect the nature of our knowledge of, and faith in, Jesus Christ.

My introductory remarks on Ernst Troeltsch in Chapter 2 reflect a fuller account of his work and significance contained in an Oxford doctoral thesis under the title of *History in the Philosophy and Theology of Ernst Troeltsch*. The account of the historical problem in Chapter 2 also refers back in part to a paper given before the Society for the Study of Theology in 1968 entitled 'Historical and Dogmatic Method in Christology'. Some of the material in Chapters 3, 4, 5, 6 took its first form in lectures given at Ripon Hall in 1968 under the Jaspers Lectureship Foundation on the theme 'In what sense may we affirm the finality of Jesus Christ?'.

The brief treatment of Teilhard's Christology in Chapter 7 really presupposes the content of three essays (published in symposia mainly devoted to the Christian–Marxist debate) in which I have tried to assess the contemporary significance of his work. The titles are: 'Marxism, Evolution and the Person of Christ', in *Evolution, Marxism and Christianity*, by Claude Cuénot and others, Garnstone Press, London, 1967; 'Teilhard de Chardin and the Christian–Marxist Dialogue', in *What Kind of Revolution?*, eds. James Klugman and Paul Oestreicher, Panther Books, London, 1968; and 'God and Man in the Christian–Marxist Dialogue', in *The Christian Marxist Dialogue*, ed. Paul Oestreicher, Macmillan, New York, 1969. My own summary view of Teilhard's thought and stature – a controversial theme – appears in *A Dictionary of Christian Theology*, ed. Alan Richardson, SCM Press, London, 1969.

Quotations from foreign authors are taken, wherever possible, from existing translations as cited in the notes. The other translations are my own.

1 The Great Breach in the Dam

Of making many books about Jesus Christ there is no end. Are these books simply going over the same ground again and again? Or is there something about the theme of 'Jesus Christ' which lends itself to unceasing comment and interpretation? At first sight the question 'Who is Jesus Christ?' is direct and simple. Moreover, there are certain 'official' answers to the question which appear to render lengthy discussion unnecessary. In the Nicene Creed, for example, we are told that Jesus Christ is:

the only-begotten Son of God,
begotten of his Father before all worlds,
God of God, Light of Light, Very God of Very God,
begotten, not made,
being of one substance with the Father,
by whom all things were made:
who for us men, and for our salvation
came down from heaven,
and was incarnate by the Holy Ghost of the Virgin Mary,
and was made man,
and was crucified also for us under Pontius Pilate.
He suffered and was buried,
and the third day he rose again
according to the scriptures, and ascended into heaven,
and sitteth on the right hand of the Father.
And he shall come again with glory
to judge both the quick and the dead:
whose kingdom shall have no end.

We may feel that such a passage deals adequately with our question about Jesus Christ. Even if these sections from the Nicene Creed can be expounded and expanded, they may already be held to constitute an answer. At this level, there is nothing especially novel or adventurous in posing again the question 'Who is Jesus Christ?'. Indeed, it smacks of the rhetorical question, favoured by preachers, which serves only as a striking introduction to an answer already known and fully prepared.

In this book I take a rather different view of the matter. I hold that the question about Jesus Christ cannot be met with a short, simple and definitive answer. I shall try to show that it is an authentic, nagging and deeply serious question from which there is no final escape. For it is a question which leads us on to a set of further questions which are vexing and stubborn in character. This means that, broadly speaking, I have to treat official statements (such as the Nicene Creed) as contributions – often invaluable – to the discussion of the question, rather than as satisfying and conclusive answers. Moreover, these vexing, stubborn and (I believe) inescapable problems concerning the question about Jesus Christ give to that discussion an ineradicably negative trait which leaves its mark upon any answer which we may frame.

I am, of course, aware that many Christians insist that the question about Jesus Christ ought to be, and can be, answered without hesitation and with considerable precision. Such people will judge that my own enquiry is marked by a tentative, provisional and sometimes sceptical spirit unacceptable to the Christian conscience. They would probably say that 'in and through Jesus Christ' is found the antidote to doubt and questioning. They would perhaps assert that, amid the changes and chances of this fleeting world, they can discover 'in Jesus Christ' a certainty as to who we are, what we need to know, what we are to do, and what we can hope for. I respect those who hold such a point of view, though I must ask whether it is securely founded. Do in fact these and other certainties really follow from what can be known about Jesus Christ? Is it possible to discover such an answer to the question about Jesus Christ whilst at the same time being truly and honestly exercised by the intractable problems which that question generates? What kind of solution to the secondary problems must be achieved if a space is to be cleared for a positive outcome to our enquiry? Or do these problems always infiltrate and harry any answer which is proposed? If this is the case, what must be said about the character of our knowledge of, and response to, the phenomenon of Jesus Christ?

On the other hand, I do not take the view that the theological enterprise concerning Jesus Christ is doomed from the outset. There are several obvious lines of approach which must be seriously and consistently explored if we are to remain at all faithful to the available data. Yet whatever approach we adopt, negative traits always emerge which build into the structure of our discussion an unavoidable inconclusiveness. This streak of negativity must be carefully examined and evaluated. On the one hand it can be treated too lightly, ignoring the fact that, for reasons which I shall discuss later, its existence and importance have become more and more obvious in recent centuries. Such cavalier treatment can lead to an assurance quickly gained but insecurely founded. On the other hand, awareness of this negativity can lead to an equally hasty and far-reaching scepticism. In my view, the Christian theologian and the Christian believer will have to probe the existence of some middle way between these two extremes. To say no more than this, however, suggests that to claim for Christianity or Jesus Christ a place 'at the centre' is a bold undertaking. In Christian devotion and in Christian theology such a central place is all too easily taken for granted without sufficient attention being paid to the factors which might count against such a claim.

A serious recognition of the negative traits in our discussion about Jesus Christ leads to our learning to stand with one foot in the camp of the unbeliever. Such a stance, once adopted, has an important bearing on how we evaluate the relation of that tradition to other traditions of thought and life.

If we evaluate the Christian tradition about Jesus Christ from the standpoint of, for example, the Nicene Creed, we are likely to imagine that a straightforward answer to the question about Jesus Christ is readily available. Rightly or wrongly, this and other official statements symbolize a monolithic view of the tradition about Jesus Christ. On this monolithic view we bring to mind that Christianity is a major world-religion of nearly two thousand years' standing, whose founder, or origin, was Jesus of Nazareth. This religion has attracted millions of adherents all owing loyalty to, and making special claims about, Jesus Christ. Throughout these centuries the Bible (regarded by many as speaking with an infallible voice), along with many other writings and artistic compositions, has borne witness to this same Jesus Christ. Similarly, we are moved to regard the unceasing and highly productive work of countless theologians over this period as variations upon a single theme. The sheer volume, richness and apparent sameness of this tradition suggests that it is no act of over-confidence to imagine that answers about Jesus Christ are within easy reach. Because so much has been said, and for so long, it is tempting to take this tradition at its face-value and to assert that the answer to our question about Jesus Christ is fully and truly given in and through that tradition. If this is a proper account of the situation, it follows that a book about Jesus Christ is more a commentary than an enquiry, more an exposition than an exploration. Seen in this light, the dissimilarities within the tradition need not cause us undue alarm. For we can easily allow that Christians and others approach this givenness in different ways and from different standpoints according to the prevailing culture, according to historical and geographical factors, and according to personal background, education and temperament. On this view there is none the less *one* tradition about Jesus Christ, for the most part compact, consistent and compelling.

This point of view is particularly persuasive for those who are bound up with the Christian community. To challenge it is to run the risk of being roughly handled by members of the church, of being treated as someone who has laid cruel and impious hands on sacred things. I want to suggest, however, that the existence of the negative traits in our discussion about Jesus Christ must cause us to look at this tradition in a very different light. I would further judge that such a new look at the tradition concerning Jesus Christ brings us face to face with a number of exceptional difficulties.

The Christian community surveys a scene in which Jesus Christ is a larger-than-life figure standing in the foreground and set against a somewhat blurred and undifferentiated background. For those who do not belong to the Christian community, this figure recedes more or less into the background. Thus, for an increasingly large portion of the world's population, it is not really a matter of moment that Christians, and Christian theologians in particular, argue ceaselessly as to what legitimately may be said about Jesus Christ. For many such people the question about Jesus Christ is marginal and alien; it belongs to the framework of a dying or dead mythology. Apart from a desire for the remembrance of things past there is now, and the 'now' refers to man in the modern age, no compelling need to attend to the fertile tradition spawned by this obsolescent mythology. The question about Jesus Christ is so limited, so peripheral, so small, so odd.

I may go to a small country parish church to seek the entry for the baptism of one I know well. In that limited setting, among people who knew that person, I can easily bring him to mind. In due course the entry leaps out at me from the appropriate page. But what of a stranger who goes to Somerset House armed with that person's name? Without any blood-tie or emotional attachment, among impersonal officials, the stranger comes upon one unimportant name among countless others. It is to this second perspective that, for many people today, the question about Jesus Christ

13

belongs. Moreover we are, for many reasons, increasingly conscious that this second perspective has its own proper validity. Jesus Christ may be the centre of our world. He is not, at least if appearances are anything to go by, the centre of any other kind of history. The tradition concerning Jesus Christ belongs, so far, to a very short period of human history. There are, moreover, certain empirical signs that the tradition is exhausting itself or being by-passed. If this were not sufficient, we have only to think in terms of biological evolution or of inter-stellar space to realize how incredibly minor and parochial, for the outsider, is the question about Jesus Christ.

It is not only that the question about Jesus Christ can appear so marginal. It is also that, to the outsider, the phenomenon of Jesus Christ seems much less detached from its environment than it seems to us. Because he is more or less central to our history, we tend to regard Jesus Christ as central to the history of others. As we look back over two thousand years, we bring into the foreground that culture and religion associated with Jesus Christ. When we speak of the medieval world, we usually have Europe in mind; we ignore China. By wrenching the tradition about Jesus Christ from its rich and complex environing context, we judge that tradition to be more unitary and monolithic than it really was or is. But if we look at that tradition from the outside, we discover that the tradition about Jesus Christ, in its brief life-span to date, belongs fairly and squarely within a subtly interwoven network of historical occurrences, affecting the latter and being affected by it. Every analysis and description which we make of that tradition is essentially an abstraction and a selection.

The Christian, along with other men, is challenged to re-nounce his intensely parochial view of the world and of history. He must in consequence find it difficult and even unconvincing to place so much weight upon one person at one point in history and in one particular place. Moreover, he lives in an era where the difficulty of such a perspective becomes daily more acute. He experiences a sharp growth in world-population and an apparent decline in numbers among supporters of the Christian religion. He experiences a growth in secular ways of life and thought, and a decline of Christian culture and ideas. All this tends to relativize the Christian phenomenon, to shift it from an apparent place at the centre to a place at *a* centre. It is not necessarily replaced by any one new centre, but assumes a position as one local centre competing with many others.

In this way we are required, looking from the outside, to view with a certain suspicion the claim that the tradition about Jesus Christ is clearly defined and monolithic in character. When such an assumption is withdrawn and when this complex historical tradition is allowed to breathe, it takes on a very different character. That such an assumption should be withdrawn is now clear. This is forced upon us not only by viewing the tradition from outside, and by viewing its close and changing connection with other traditions. It is forced upon us also by virtue of the work which has been done internally by theologians in respect of the tradition about Jesus Christ. Through the work of biblical scholars, through the work of historians of the tradition, and through those who have studied the environment of the tradition at different points in time, it has now become necessary to talk of an incredibly diverse and heterogeneous tradition. Nor can this diversity be simply attributed to divergencies from a norm or norms. Indeed, recent theological debate has shown how difficult it is to speak of norms, or of developments within the tradition. For which tradition among the traditions is to be called the norm, and who is to arbitrate among the claimants? It is extremely difficult to decide on relevant critieria for such an enterprise. Moreover, it has become increasingly clear that the source of this diversity lies not least with the very varied cultural patterns within which the Christian community finds itself. This applies, of course, as much to the cultural context in which the New Testament documents arose as it does to any other period in Christian history. A classic example of the way in which the diversity of the Christian tradition can be demonstrated is found in Ernst Troeltsch's *The Social Teaching of the Christian Churches*.[1] This is a remarkable survey of Christian social teaching from the early church to modern times. Troeltsch showed that it is impossible to discover any *one* pattern of social teaching. There is instead an incredible diversity produced by the very different social environments in which that teaching has been formulated. The German title (*Die Soziallehren*), which has 'Teachings' rather than 'Teaching', describes more accurately the contents and the conclusion of the work!

I have already emphasized that our insight into the diversity of the Christian tradition in general, and of the tradition about Jesus Christ in particular, is to some extent of modern origin. I shall discuss this in detail at a later stage. For the present it is sufficient to observe two of the factors which have led to our fuller discernment of this diversity. The first and positive factor, already mentioned, lies with the growth of historical consciousness about the cultural environment of the Christian tradition at its various stages. The second and negative factor lies with the erosion of the different authorities which are appealed to in support of this or that stage of the tradition. On the one hand there has been the appeal to the Bible as the norm of the tradition. This appeal has been grounded in some theory of biblical inspiration which guarantees the biblical text as an authoritative source for the making of Christian doctrine. On the other hand, norms have been established by appeal to a text or statement which is given authoritative status by an ecclesiastical body. Historical-critical study of the Bible has undermined once and for all the former approach. There is no doubt that the biblical writings must be accorded a special and significant status in respect of the question about Jesus Christ. This status derives, however, from what the texts contain rather than from any theory about their provenance which may be imposed upon them from without. Similarly, an appeal to the Thirty-Nine Articles, to the Augsburg Confession, to the Council of Trent or to the Council of Chalcedon as guarantors of a doctrinal norm must be regarded with suspicion. For, once the authority of the bodies which issued such statements is no longer taken on trust but is subjected to critical scrutiny, we are left with the search for criteria which guarantee those bodies as guarantors of norms.

The last two centuries or so have seen the virtual collapse of these authorities. They linger on in some quarters, but it is hard to see how they can carry weight for much longer with any substantial number of people. We can variously designate the present era as one in which competing and even conflicting authorities seem to cancel one another out, as one in which new forms of authority are being sought, or as one in which some Christians seek to live out and understand their faith without appeal to formal authorities. This is a complex, and probably only an interim, state of affairs. Be that as it may, it only serves to highlight that diversity which has always belonged to the Christian tradition, but which has, at some times more than others, been hidden or restricted by the weight of ecclesiastical authority.

The recognition of this diversity does not commit us at the same time to saying that one part of the tradition is as good as another. It does, however, require us to be extremely cautious about the decisions which we make in this respect. For the dominance of a particular strand of the tradition at any one point in time may be due as much to earthy political and social factors as to delicate spiritual insight. We may seek to avoid this sort of problem by insisting that Christian discrimination in this regard is guided by the Holy Spirit. There is no need to deny the possibility of such guidance. But it is extraordinarily difficult to determine on what grounds we should wish to affirm the working of the Holy Spirit in one case and not in another. This kind of argument, just because of its looseness and comprehensive character,

17

must be employed (if at all) only with very great care.

How, then, are we to handle this diversity of reflection in the tradition about Jesus Christ? This is an important and searching question which deserves careful attention. For the answers which we give at this stage will largely determine the use to which we put the tradition and thus will shape the answer which we construct. To illustrate the problem, I will suggest six alternative approaches to this diversity.

1. Each element, or each major element, within the diversity of the tradition about Jesus Christ contributes part of the answer which we seek. The answer is found nowhere entire; each element reveals a fragment of that answer. An example of this approach may be found in the litany much used in ecumenical circles where God is thanked for the particular aspect of the truth of the Christian gospel enshrined in each denominational tradition. This theory seems to presuppose that we know, from some independent source or another, what the Christian gospel in fact is. It presupposes that we can speak of this gospel, on independent evidence, with sufficient precision to be able to identify its parts in the ethos and belief of the various denominations.

2. Only one element within the diversity contains the answer. The other moments of the tradition are more or less mistaken. In the first approach which we discussed, diversity was seen as a strength – even as a necessity. In this second approach it must be regarded as a sign of weakness, of muddle-headedness, even of a wilful and sin-laden refusal to see the light. Here again we need to know in advance what the gospel is, or we must at least be sure that we have confidence in the voice which claims to be the arbiter of truth. Thus we are taken back to the need for criteria by which this claim can be defended or refuted. This applies as much to the teaching magisterium of the Roman Catholic Church as it does to Mary Baker Eddy.

3. In each element of the diverse tradition about Jesus

Christ is found a kernel of truth common to all. However varied the husks may be, if removed they will reveal in each case one and the same answer. A version of this thesis may be found in the notion of an 'essence of Christianity' popularized by Harnack and others. In another version, it leads to a syncretistic faith which seeks the highest common factor in different religions or different denominations. In practice we need to ask how the kernel is in fact identified in the first place and how far the extraction of this kernel does justice or violence to the overall context in which it belongs.

4. No element in the diversity of the tradition about Jesus Christ contains either a part or a whole of the answer. Nor do the many elements amalgamate to form an answer. Nevertheless, some or all of these elements somehow point beyond themselves to an answer dimly discerned but never fully grasped. This thesis appears to respect the cultural conditionedness of each element. But it is not clear as to how we even begin to know what is being pointed to.

5. The diversity of the tradition about Jesus Christ is somehow processive in character. Through an organic development, whether in a crude orthogenetic evolution or through some tortuous dialectic, the answer is slowly being fashioned. But it will be available and verifiable only at the end. This thesis has a pleasing aspect. For it appears to allow the diversity to be truly what it is. On the other hand, the thesis also implies that there is a beginning and an end. This is either known independently or it has somehow come to light in what we already know about the process itself. If the latter is in fact the case, we cannot assume that there will be an end. We can only extrapolate from the present, and frame the hypothesis that there might be an end.

6. The diversity of the tradition about Jesus Christ is such that no answer at all is possible. There remains only a set of conflicting proposals for which we have no standards of measurement. The way is left open for an extreme relativism, for a tentative personal belief which respects all

other beliefs, for a 'truth for me' which can be either elegiac, promethean or fanatical in style.

There are arguments for and against all these gambits. Some are mutually exclusive, others are not. How are we to choose among them? If there is no *a priori* authority to dictate our choice, we are left with the question: 'To which of these gambits does the evidence point?' While I am convinced that this is the proper, and indeed the only approach to the problem, I am also clear that the notion of evidence constitutes a vexing problem on its own account. For the notion of evidence can apply in three senses to the question about the diversity of the tradition concerning Jesus Christ. In the first place we have the problem of the evidence concerning Jesus of Nazareth as a human agent at a particular point in time and place in history. In the second place there is the tradition about him which, as I have already suggested, does not appear to contain its own canons of interpretation. In the third place there is evidence in the sense of our own attitudes to the world, and thus to questions about knowledge and truth, which shape our response to the first two categories of evidence mentioned above. Moreover, these are three areas of evidence are closely related to each other; no one of them can be looked at in isolation.

We must therefore face up to the fact that any answer which can be given to the question about Jesus Christ must emerge from a veritable maze of reflection. The outlook is not, however, as gloomy as it may seem, since certain signposts are available within the maze. Moreover, we do not have to assume that there is only one way through the maze. I am, of course, aware that there are many people who would insist that my account of things is too complicated, and would hold that access to Jesus Christ can be achieved more directly. Yet I believe that most of the arguments which are used in support of such short-cuts are open to severe criticism.

Perhaps the most appealing of these arguments is the one which claims that, precisely so that we do not have to be entangled in the maze which I have described, God has vouchsafed to us in Jesus Christ a revelation, and has vouchsafed to us an interior capacity for response to that revelation, by virtue of which we are not dependent upon our normal ways of knowing. This is certainly an attractive theory, but I am by no means clear that it can be readily accepted. If the theory is acceptable, then we need have no problems in respect of the diversity within the tradition about Jesus Christ. For every item in this tradition could be tested by reference to this revelation. In recent theological discussion the notion of revelation has been widely canvassed, though it has not become clear exactly what is being claimed, nor has the basis of those claims been clearly expounded. The problem is as to what constitutes this revelation, given that we cannot make a simple appeal to either Bible or church as guarantors of, or spokesmen for, this revelation.

If the revelation theory cannot be used, then we are forced back upon the problem of the diversity of the tradition about Jesus Christ, and upon the need to find our way round that diversity without special help. In other words, our search has to begin 'from below' with the three areas of evidence which I have already mentioned. This is a decisive step in the discussion, since we can already surmise that the approach 'from below' will certainly not supply us with secure and easily verifiable answers about Jesus Christ.

I take the view that we cannot in fact *begin* our enquiry about Jesus Christ from a supposed revelation. It is important to state at this stage why I believe that this move is not legitimate. The American theologian Carl Braaten, following Paul Althaus, has recently spoken of the 'inflation of revelation'. He refers critically to the

widespread assumption in Protestant theology that the idea of revelation itself most comprehensively and most profoundly expresses the

21

uniqueness of the Christian faith. Every modern Protestant theology . . . has felt obliged to establish itself as a theology of revelation, as if thereby it has achieved all that matters or what matters most.[2]

These remarks by Braaten only summarize a growing sense of misgiving about the notion of revelation. Similar hesitations have been voiced by Gerald Downing, James Barr, John McIntyre and others. Downing asks whether the phrase 'the revelation of God in Christ' is either a meaningful or a biblical idea. He concludes that for the most part it is not a biblical idea, if we mean by revelation what many contemporary theologians take it to mean, namely the making clear of something that is hidden. Thus Downing concludes that:

the New Testament talks rather . . . of what God has done and is doing. Already we are 'redeemed', 'accepted', 'made holy'. This is as sure and complete as the Cross and Resurrection and presence of the Spirit. It is final. But 'revelation' cannot yet be said to be complete; it is barely begun; it is, we may believe, the ultimate but still very incomplete aim of what God has already done, and still does.[3]

Concerning the meaning of revelation, Downing asserts that:

the theologian is using a word that normally describes 'making clear' to mean 'leave unclear'. . . . If God intended to 'reveal himself' in Christ, in the events of his life and death and resurrection and in his teaching, he failed. . . . That he intends finally to 'reveal himself' to us we may well hope.[4]

Downing is saying that there is in fact such poor, disputed and limited knowledge of God in evidence that we are forced to qualify the notion of revelation with a word such as 'partial'. In doing this we destroy the concept of revelation.

In some respects McIntyre only repeats Downing's analysis. I want, however, to summarize one of his main conclusions, since it points out very clearly the dangers inherent in an over-dependence on the notion of revelation.

Revelation is not a theological conjuror's hat out of which we may draw the rabbits of the several doctrines of the Christian faith.[5]

The notion of revelation stands too low on the hierarchy of theological models for that to be the case. Thus we have to say that Jesus Christ is the revelation of God (third-order statement) because he is God incarnate (second-order statement) because he fulfilled all God's promises to Israel (first-order statement).

Barr has some comments about the notion of revelation which are complementary to those of Downing and McIntyre. He observes that it can obstruct and distort the empirical analysis of biblical texts. If we bring to these texts an already formed concept of revelation, we tend to make the context conform to the concept. This leads to a reduction in exegetical sharpness, and to a rather blurred patterning of the biblical evidence. In the second place, Barr notes that the category of revelation is often opposed to that of 'religion'. Among writers who do this, one exception is usually made to the rule – namely biblical religion. Since revelation is closely linked with the Bible, there is a tendency to devalue non-biblical Christianity and other religions and to overvalue biblical religion. Barr, on the other hand, judges that it is incorrect to treat biblical religion in isolation from other religious currents of the time. For we thereby deny that 'important elements in what later was the Israelite tradition emerged from the Near Eastern environment'.[6] This is a point of considerable importance which I have already mentioned in a general way. A full stress on the cultural conditionedness of the biblical tradition makes it difficult to draw convenient lines around an area of revelation. As Barr succinctly comments:

the appropriation of environing material is of such importance as to call for a positive theological statement.[7]

I want now to suggest one reason why this rather fragile notion of revelation has become so dominant. I shall try to show that it has come to the fore as a response to a genuine difficulty in which Christian theology has found itself. If, however, we agree to any appreciable extent with

23

the queries raised against this notion by the authors mentioned, then we are still left with that difficulty and must discover better ways of coping with it.

Barr noted that the dominance of the concept of revelation is a modern phenomenon. It now has a function which it never had in the whole previous history of the church. The same point has been made by Downing and others. In fact the modern emphasis on revelation probably dates from the Enlightenment and attains to full dominance only in the last hundred years. This rise of the notion of revelation coincides, roughly speaking, with a fundamental and comparatively sudden intellectual change in the Western world. The dating of this change is not important, though it is probably correct to say that the great breach in the dam took place only in the seventeenth and eighteenth centuries.[8] Troeltsch outlined the content of this change in the following way:

> . . . the shattering of the ideal presuppositions and contents of the ecclesiastical world-view. A new cosmology and anthropology, a critical science of history, a humanitarian ethic shattered its whole existence, its formal authority of revelation and its actual convictions. Under these circumstances the general sense of self-evidentness of the church's cultural presuppositions disappears and a major part of the most lively spiritual culture is thus unchurched.[9]

In turn, Gerhard Ebeling has tried to describe the common factor which 'fundamentally and irrevocably marks off the modern age as a whole from all preceding Western history'.[10] Ebeling suggests that in the modern age the Christian faith has forfeited the self-evident validity that was ascribed to it in Western history for more than a millennium. It is no longer accorded any formal authority which stands *extra controversiam*. In consequence, all metaphysical statements are eliminated from the realm of the self-evident and neither the church nor any world-view that supposes itself absolute may be allowed to question the relative autonomy of science and of social life. This is a fundamental change never to be unmade.

There is no doubt that this loss of self-evident validity has constituted a major crisis for Christian theology, all of whose affirmations are now exposed to controversy. Thus the history of Christian theology in the last three centuries may, for the greater part, be not unfairly described as a series of retreating retaliations to that crisis. One attempt after another has been made by Christian theology to lay claim to an authority which could guarantee its validity. As one area after another has been surrendered to controversy, repeated attempts have been made to negotiate and to consolidate new demilitarized zones which will be immune from criticism. Obviously the Bible played an important part in this process. Theories of its formal authority have been slowly whittled away so that it must today seem a far cry from the time when a Protestant scholastic theologian could describe the Bible as 'part of God'. It is within this overall process that the notion of revelation has been introduced as a device by which a stable foundation may be supplied for Christian thought and life. It has been thought that the notion of revelation could provide a means whereby all proper concessions could be made to scientific knowledge, where historical-critical work on the Bible could be responsibly taken into account, but also where faith could have its own proper object free from the incursions of critical thought. The modern concept of revelation represents perhaps the most ambitious of a number of attempts that have been made to set up an iron curtain between what is known by reason and what is experienced by faith. Unfortunately, as we have seen, the notion of revelation is too shadowy and derivative in character to sustain this high calling.

It has therefore been borne upon us ever more clearly that Christian faith, and with it Christian theology, must finally surrender its claims both to self-evident validity and to a validity guaranteed by an authority which somehow stands above those criteria of truthfulness which are in common use. Thus, not without reason, theology finds itself today both hesitant and insecure. For theology has now to take fully into account, as I indicated at the beginning of this

25

chapter, not only a general critical climate about its subject matter but also certain particular criticisms which cannot easily be shaken off. This means that a long and rich theological tradition of more than sixteen hundred years must be approached with presuppositions in many respects quite different from those of the people who constructed that tradition.

That this situation has occasioned a failure of nerve on the part of Christian theology is beyond dispute. It has led, for example, to a scepticism about theology among many who profess Christian belief, to a consciously anti-theological embrace of 'pure faith', mysticism, social action, etc. It has fostered, among those who remain within the theological fold, a tendency whereby theology is broken down into its sub-disciplines, all of which can claim responsibility by virtue of their association with existing secular disciplines, and which can be strenuously pursued without reference to wider questions. It has encouraged a reversion to various kinds of theological authoritarianism. It has stimulated that disastrous reductionism by which, in one way or another, theological statements are held to be 'no more than' statements about man. These are understandable reactions. For, even after three hundred years or more, I suspect that we have hardly yet begun to come to terms with what is involved in this loss of self-evident validity and in the parallel rise of the autonomy of man, i.e. of what Bonhoeffer described as the 'discovery of the laws by which the world lives and deals with itself in science, social and political matters, art, ethics, and religion'.[11] Perhaps the most significant example of the time-lag between the onset of this loss of self-evident validity and our appreciation of its significance for theology lies in the field of historical-critical work on the Bible. Although this work began in earnest at the end of the eighteenth century, it is fair to say that its significance for theological construction is still not fully explored. This exploration has undoubtedly been held up by the perhaps natural desire of churchmen to protect their Christian faith against suspected erosion. There is therefore, all in all, a sense in which theology may in fact be said to be standing on the threshold of an era quite different from that in which much of its creative work was done.

At an earlier point in this chapter I outlined some of the different approaches which are possible towards the rich diversity which marks the theological tradition about Jesus Christ. I suggested there that in choosing our way we must above all be attentive to evidence; to the evidence we have about Jesus, to the evidence of the theological tradition about him, and to the evidence which comes from the understanding which we have of our world. This is essentially an open approach, and one that is required of us in view of the loss of self-evident validity on the part of Christian faith. In the following chapters I shall try to exhibit some of the positive and negative features which emerge when such an enquiry is set in motion. It is impossible to attain to any degree of comprehensiveness in such an enterprise. I cannot, therefore, take more than the very first steps in the search for answers to the question about Jesus Christ. At the present time, however, I regard it as far more important that we should become as aware as we possibly can of some of the difficulties and the possibilities which that question evokes. For I shall conclude that the most significant feature of our answer to the question about Jesus Christ is precisely its fragmentary, inconclusive and paradoxical character.

NOTES

1. Translated by Olive Wyon, 2 vols., London 1931.

2. *History and Hermeneutic*, London 1968, pp. 11 f.

3. F. G. Downing, *Has Christianity a Revelation?*, London 1964, pp. 124 f.

4. *Op. cit.*, p. 238.

5. John McIntyre, *The Shape of Christology*, London 1966, p. 168.

6. James Barr, *Old and New in Interpretation*, London 1966, p. 98.

7. *Ibid.*

8. G. Ebeling, *Word and Faith*, London 1963, p. 43.

9. E. Troeltsch, *Die Trennung von Staat und Kirche*, Tübingen 1907, pp. 25 f.

10. Ebeling, *op. cit.*, p. 43.

11. D. Bonhoeffer, *Letters and Papers from Prison*, second revised edition, London 1967, p. 178.

2 The Critical Canons of Historical Thinking

I want now to begin a closer analysis of what is involved in asking the question about Jesus Christ by drawing attention to a problem which has become of special significance in recent centuries, and which now dogs any steps which we may want to take in the task of theological construction. This is, of course, the 'problem of history'. Broadly speaking, it can be said that Christian theology has claimed that in certain events associated with Jesus Christ, and in some other events too, God has acted (or manifested himself) in a quite remarkable way towards man.

> However, with the development of historical-critical tools of inquiry and their application to the historical foundations of Christian faith, difficult new problems have forced themselves upon the attention of the church in its efforts to maintain and clarify the meaning of this conviction ... Must the Christian church, in order to hold fast to its historical consciousness, subject its heritage to the more precise and critical canons of modern historical thinking?[1]

We are concerned, then, with particular historical problems and their impact upon the continuing work of theology, but we may also legitimately speak of the 'problem of history', in the general sense that modern historical consciousness brings an entirely new dimension to the theological undertaking. In order to set the historical issue in proper perspective, we must operate at both these levels. And at both levels it soon becomes clear that the historical problem constitutes one of those negative traits in our handling of the question concerning Jesus Christ which I mentioned in the first chapter. For the historical problem is, both thematically and as a stage in the history of ideas, closely bound up with the loss of self-evident validity to which I earlier referred. It is one of the main features of that intellectual change never to be unmade.

In discussing that loss of self-evident validity, I remarked on the strange mixture of positive and negative traits which is entailed. On the one hand, it *has* led to the fuller 'discovery of the laws by which the world lives and deals with itself', which must surely be regarded as fruitful for theology in one way or another. On the other hand, it has helped to usher in and to accelerate the process of secularization understood in the straightforward sense of 'the transition from beliefs and activities and institutions presupposing beliefs of a traditional Christian kind to beliefs and activities and institutions of an atheistic kind'.[2] Likewise, historical science has enabled theology to make tremendous strides in the handling of its sources, but, as we shall see, has had to pay a price for this which many theologians have regarded as too high. Moreover, the historical question is of exceptional importance in the quest for Jesus Christ, since it raises very sharply from one particular direction the question which I mentioned more generally in my first chapter, namely, the determining of starting-points for that quest.

I shall outline what are, I believe, some of the main issues in this respect by reference to the work of one thinker, most of whose intellectual energies were in one way or another devoted to a consideration of this theme. He is Ernst Troeltsch (1865–1923), a German scholar who was active in the fields of history, philosophy and theology. Following his own pattern of thinking, I shall first set the historical question in a broad context. I shall then explain what, according to Troeltsch, are the resultant challenges for the theologian.

Troeltsch would readily concur with the judgement that the really new element in the thought of today as compared with that of three centuries ago is the rise of history.[3] This historical revolution is, moreover, of a radical kind, requiring us to consider anew all our presuppositions about man and the world. As F. R. Tennant has said:

the historical movement has exerted a determinative influence upon thought and investigation comparable in importance with that of Newtonian science and the Copernican revolution.[4]

Troeltsch took the view that this revolution had begun in the eighteenth century as a product of the Enlightenment and had then gained momentum under the influence of the Romantic movement. By the nineteenth century it could, however, be said that historical science

has so fully and so thoroughly worked out the genesis of our civilization, and has so made all present conditions intelligible by tracing the history of their development, that all thinking is obliged to become in some measure historical, and that this knowledge is an essential part of the equipment of all attempts to modify present conditions.[5]

I shall not in this context attempt to analyse the discussion and debate which has ranged around judgements such as these. I shall instead draw attention to what Troeltsch discerned as the two main features in this new understanding of history, both of which ultimately affect the theological enterprise.

The first of these is the notion of 'individuality'. This idea, which has been traced back to Leibnitz and others, gained a new historical dimension in the period mentioned above. Thus towards the end of the eighteenth century:

the cosmical order was coming to be conceived not as an infinite static diversity, but as a process of increasing diversification ... There have, in the entire history of thought, been few changes in standards of value more profound and more momentous than that which took place when the contrary principle began to prevail – when it came to be believed not only that in many, or in all, phases of human life there are diverse excellences, but that diversity itself is of the essence of excellence.[6]

Profoundly influenced by Friedrich Schleiermacher and

Wilhelm Dilthey, Troeltsch took up this notion of historical individuality at two levels, analytical and speculative, and though these are closely related, it is the first which here mainly concerns us. With the notion of individuality Troeltsch believed that he had found an analytical tool which could do full justice to the richness and diversity of cultural history, and could rescue the latter from servitude to the methods of the natural sciences. When the historian looks at the past he deals not with a separate 'element', as popular science has understood the basic unit of physical reality, but with an 'individual totality'. The latter is given expression as the result of an act of intuitive abstraction or selection by the historian. For history does not present to us simple units, but:

> magnitudes which have already coalesced . . . in which an abundance of psychical elemental occurrences, together with certain natural conditions, are always already clustered together in a unity of life or totality.[7]

It is not that the historian adds together a number of items to manufacture such a unity of life. He rather intuits these unities of life in the material before him. These individual totalities do not usually turn out to be human individuals in the narrow sense, but more and more 'collective individualities' (nations, classes, cultural eras, etc.). Thus a totality can be defined as that which can be abstracted from the flow of events by virtue of the fact that it can be surveyed as a unit possessing a certain compactness. The precise lines of demarcation for such units will always be difficult to sketch in, and depend to a great extent upon the skill and sensitivity of the historian.

Troeltsch develops this notion of individual totality in a number of interesting directions. In particular, he emphasizes that the historian, in attempting to grasp and to isolate the totality, is always involved in a process of selection. He cannot, of course, extract the desired totality as it stands from the flow of events. He has therefore to draw out those traits which are characteristic of the totality. This means that the selection which the historian finally achieves can never consist in more than representative or symbolizing examples.

The second main concept in Troeltsch's understanding of history is 'development'. He writes:

> Thus the fundamental concept of historical individuality brings with it the concept of the continuous connection of being or, as most people today are accustomed to say, of development.[8]

In the first place it must be made clear that 'development' or 'becoming' is not tied, in Troeltsch's scheme, to any evolutionary world-view. Both words are somewhat misleading in this respect. As we shall see, Troeltsch refers for the most part to the connections which obtain within the historical process. The individual totality, we noted, was a construction by the historian of a unity of life which presented itself to him in his material. He selects from the flux of phenomena that which is qualitatively individual. This is not an arbitrary act, a forcing of the material, since historical phenomena do in fact manifest their own compactness, novelty and other traits. Thus far Troeltsch has made no judgement about the way in which one individual totality is related to another, nor indeed has he said much about the relations which obtain within an individual totality.

By having recourse to the notion of development, Troeltsch shows that the individual totality does not exhaustively describe the nature of that which the historian has before him in his sources. For with development, understood as a continuous connection of becoming, Troeltsch adds to the notion of individual totality the sense of *movement* which belongs to the historical process. When the historian, struck by the overall compactness and coherence of a bunch of occurrences, abstracts and seeks to depict an individual totality, he is abstracting from movement in general, from the general flow of becoming. Thus the totality is both part of a process and a process in its own right.[9]

It is, however, for our purposes extremely important also to note the wider sense of 'development' as referring to the relations between totalities. The totality is a 'segment of life',[10] i.e., a part, however compact, of general historical agitation and fluidity. There is therefore no such thing as an isolated complex of development. The latter always blurs into surrounding phenomena at the edges. One complex of development is related to, and can never really be separated from, other proximate complexes of development and surrounding historical movement in general. Thus the notion of development draws attention to the continuity which exists between the cultural creations of the human spirit in different eras and places. However complex and virtually indescribable this continuity may be, it nonetheless points to the fact that one historical circle of development is to a high degree shaped and created by one or more circles which precede and surround it.

The notion of development also confirms the point which Troeltsch made in his account of individuality, namely that the latter very rarely refers to an isolated event or person, but nearly always to a larger complex. Certainly Troeltsch's use of 'individual' is never numerical but is a qualitative judgement about the essential trait of a totality. This means that the historian is not concerned with isolated events, though it does not, of course, mean that the historian can treat lightly what are usually called 'facts'. Development thus emphasizes that the historical unit is not just an individuality but an individuality-process. And it is impossible to intuit the essential trait of this process from a single event, even though there may be many strong personalities and decisive events which materially shape the structure of a certain circle of development.

In the preceding paragraphs I have only discussed those aspects of Troeltsch's treatment of individuality and develop-

34

ment which have a close bearing upon the theological enterprise. I shall now describe how Troeltsch himself effects this transition.

Troeltsch saw the historical revolution as part of a fundamental transformation of our knowledge in methods and results. As far as theology was concerned, this led to the scientific shattering of the fundamental ideas of earlier Christianity.[11] Christian theology could no longer reasonably claim immunity from general historical methods. We must instead allow that historical science determines theology, and not vice versa. Troeltsch goes on to propose the thesis that historical science, with its categories of individuality and development, damages beyond repair the supernaturalist framework in which much Christian theology has been set. Troeltsch is not out to reject supernaturalism as such, but rather what he calls 'the supernatural which exists only in Christianity' or again 'an entirely idiosyncratic causality of revelation proper only to Christianity'.[12] He explains that he is forced to this rejection of special supernaturalism in view of the impact which the historical-critical method has had upon him. In part he means that a theory of supernaturalism cannot be based on uncertain facts of history, forasmuch as 'we catch sight of the personality of Jesus only through the veil of a tradition which conceals ... basic ... matters'.[13]

This is not, however, the main burden of his criticism. It is rather that when the historical-critical method is admitted, no boundaries can be drawn in respect of its operation. When this method is applied to the New Testament, for example, it emerges that there is:

an interweaving of Christian and extra-Christian material, a dependence upon the total situation. To be sure this does not remove Christianity's autonomy; it rather reveals it as a phenomenon with extraordinary powers of assimilation. But it does render impossible a separation of natural and supernatural components, a distinction between that which is humanly conditioned and that which is directly divine.[14]

35

If this is the case, it follows that the narrower work of historical criticism, namely to ascertain the historicity of particular events, is not of primary importance. Nor, when Troeltsch cites 'religious-historical studies' as the reason for his rejection of exclusive supernaturalism, is he primarily referring to the available results of the comparative-historical study of particular religions. Rather, it already follows from what he has said about individuality and development that we must speak of the 'interweaving of Christian and extra-Christian material'.

Certainly Troeltsch's reading of what was going on in the History-of-Religions school of his day only confirmed this thesis. Indeed, Troeltsch thought that the main yield from the work of historical theology in the nineteenth century lay in the demonstration that Christianity must now be seen in its origins and development as inextricably intertwined with the whole context of historical life, as conditioned in a variety of ways by its environment and as set in the whole stream of historical becoming. The contemporary study of Christian origins confirmed this thesis for him in the sense that it illustrated his contention that within any individual totality each event is horizontally related to, and partly dependent on, others around it. In turn each individual totality is horizontally related to others in a network of development. It is therefore impossible for the historian to conceive of single events of an exclusively supernatural kind, since no one event can be exclusive of any other. This does not exclude novelty from history; it does, however, mean that novelty is always in part dependent upon that which precedes and surrounds it.

The theological implications of these ideas are worked out by Troeltsch, with some care but not in any great detail, in his essay 'On Historical and Dogmatic Method in Theology'.[15] This essay was a response to a previous essay by a writer who had tried to cope with the historical challenge in a piecemeal way to avoid having to surrender exclusive supernaturalism. Troeltsch holds that this is impossible, since the historical method is a leaven which transforms everything and which finally explodes entirely the theological method hitherto known.

Troeltsch observes that theological method starts at a point outside history from which it derives certain unconditional propositions. At this initial and crucial point, theology is immune from historical criticism. Beginning its work in this way, theology goes on to postulate certain 'events' which do not belong to ordinary history, inasmuch as they can be neither established nor refuted by historical criticism, but are guaranteed as to their status by an appeal to miracle or by some similar device. Theological method cannot allow these 'events' to be subjected to historical criticism:

(*a*) because it could not accept for these events the inevitable conclusion of historical method that their historicity is at best probable but never certain;

(*b*) because in seeking to establish their historicity historical criticism would appeal, on the basis of analogy, to other events of an apparently similar kind, whereas the theologian (on the other hand) is claiming *a priori* that these events are unique;

(*c*) because to hand over these 'events' to historical method would involve their insertion into the whole network of empirical occurrence with its principle of reciprocal causality, whereas these 'events' (it is held) follow a different, spiritual law of causality. Thus, although the theological method purports to deal with certain 'historical events', these turn out to be events of a very special kind. They are events in a history of salvation and can only really be recognized by the believer. The theory of a history of salvation claims that absolute divine truth is concentrated in certain events, whereas ordinary history deals only with events which are conditioned by other events and so cannot, in consequence, possess any such absoluteness.

In consequence the dogmatic approach flies in the face of

historical method with its three characteristic notes of 'criticism', 'analogy' and 'correlation'. 'Acclimatization to the principle of historical criticism' means that in the area of history we must allow that judgements can never be more than judgements of greater or lesser probability. These judgements, whatever degree of probability they attain at any one time, must be continually submitted to the ongoing and changing work of historians. But in what way are such judgements of probability even possible? How is the historian to bridge the gulf of time which separates him from his material? Here Troeltsch appeals to the concept of analogy as an essential feature of the historical method, though of course supported by the scholarly apparatus of the professional historian. Troeltsch has two versions of analogy in mind. The first enables us to reconstruct the past by analogy with the present. The second enables us to reconstruct one historical entity by analogy with another. The first of these is always prior. For only by analogy with phenomena which occur in and around us can we recognize similar phenomena in historical material, and so attest their probability. Thus, the extent to which we ascribe probability to past phenomena depends for the most part on how far they accord with the 'normal, usual, or at least widely attested, modes of occurrence and circumstances that we know'.[16] Only when this has happened can we take the process one stage further and observe analogies between past phenomena, so that uncertain features of one may be judged by analogy with the more certain features of another.

This doctrine of analogy presupposes a homogeneity between historical phenomena. It is not that all historical reality is to be treated as uniform, but that there is some common factor by which genuine similarities can be approached and, in part, grasped. It is in this context that Troeltsch discusses 'correlation', as referring to this interconnection between phenomena.

Troeltsch can now therefore assert that:

the historical method leads, by criticism, analogy and correlation ...

to the recovery of a mutually-conditioned network of expressions of the human spirit – expressions which are at no point absolute or isolated, but rather stand everywhere connected.[17]

From this picture of historical method, Troeltsch makes three parallel inferences about theological method:

1. Religious tradition is subject to the same canons of probability as any other historical tradition.

2. Religious tradition can only be understood by analogy with other historical traditions past and present.

3. Religious tradition can only become comprehensible when it is seen in reciprocal connection with the whole religious and cultural history of mankind. Thus Troeltsch concludes:

If this is the way things are, then only one conclusion can be drawn. The historical method must be used with the fullest seriousness. It is not simply a matter of recognizing the relative uncertainty of all historical knowledge, of appreciating that the connection of religious faith to individual historical facts is a relative and mediate connection, of subjecting clearly and decisively Jewish-Christian history to the consequences of a historical method without fear for, or evasion of, the results. Above all, it is a matter of recognizing the involvement of Christianity in history in general and of attending to the task of its investigation and evaluation only from the context of total history. The historical method must be pursued in theology with full and un-prejudiced consistency.[18]

I do not wish to suggest that Troeltsch's analysis of the historical problem is complete or that his proposals must be accepted without demur. He has, however, highlighted certain problems which remain with us today, sometimes in an even more acute form. For Troeltsch was one of the first to ask really probing questions about the relationship of historical-critical work to theological construction. The effect of his labours was to show that, once the Christian tradition (including the biblical writings) is opened up to historical analysis, certain consequences follow which are at first sight alarming for the theologian. It is quite clear that Troeltsch's handling of this problem was inadequate in a number of ways. All the same, many of his questions have to some extent been left in abeyance despite the fact that actual historical-critical work has proceeded apace since his day. This point has been emphasized by Ebeling in the context of some general remarks about the destinies of theology in the nineteenth and twentieth centuries. Ebeling writes:

> It is a real question, however, whether the relationship to the nineteenth century does not require to be more carefully considered and reviewed also at *the* very points on which there is today a widespread conviction of having reached a final judgement. . . . It would be an illusion to hold that this crisis (of the late nineteenth century) . . . has been overcome. For all the anti-historical reactions that have appeared are unserviceable attempts to settle the problem it has brought.[19]

Another German writer has made a similar point, but more positively, about Troeltsch himself:

> Ernst Troeltsch perceived, like no other theologian of his time, the upsetting and urgent features of the problem about the relation between faith and history. No one else posed such profound and serious questions about the significance of the historical method for theology.[20]

To conclude this chapter I want first to extract two particular points from Troeltsch's account of the historical problem. In the second place, I shall offer some general remarks about the relationship of history to theology as these arise from Troeltsch's overall undertaking.

Troeltsch's main thesis is that, when historical data are in question, theology may not proceed without reference to the work of historical science. Moreover, he takes the view that historical science, when it is asked to give an account of itself, will not allow that theology can appeal to particular events as mediating a special and unique divine action. We may not classify some events as being of a normal earthly character, while other events are given a miraculous status. Troeltsch rejects such a theory on the grounds that all events are linked together laterally in a way that precludes our giving to one event an independence through some direct, vertical link with God. It is in consequence not

40

legitimate to draw a circle around a certain set of events and to call them a history of salvation. For in this way we artificially separate certain events from other surrounding events which in part make the former what they are. I observed in the previous chapter that Barr made a similar point when he remarked on the problem caused by the fact that biblical religion drew on environing material in the making of its tradition.

It seems that to some extent modern theology has taken account of this difficulty. Less and less emphasis, for example, has been laid on particular events in Jesus' life; more and more attention has been paid to his total life. Likewise the arena of God's saving acts has been carried backwards into the Old Testament history and forwards into the history of the early church. But if Troeltsch's thesis is at all valid, we can only regard these moves as evasions of the real issue. For at what point are we to draw the lines in order to state unequivocally that this event belongs to the class of divine acts whereas that event does not? Troeltsch held that no such line could be drawn. Everything in the biblical tradition and beyond is an 'expression of the human spirit'. It is true that Troeltsch, who was a theist, believed that the human spirit can be everywhere open to the promptings of the divine life. This does not, however, mean that any single event can lay claim to direct divine causation.

Thus we are led again to the point which I raised in the first chapter. On what grounds may we choose to curtail the incursions of historical science at particular points? To negate Troeltsch's thesis we have to find a means whereby we can somehow guarantee that certain events do belong to a special salvation history and are not available for historical-critical inspection. To do this we must in turn be able to turn to some authority which can perform this function for us. But where, in the age of the loss of self-evident validity and of the erosion of formal authorities, are we to find a candidate for this role?

This takes us on to Troeltsch's secondary thesis concerning

the element of probability in all our historical judgements. Troeltsch was, I believe, correct in not exalting this question to undue prominence. It is nonetheless of considerable importance, for, at the end of the day, it means that all the historical judgements on which the theologian seeks to build are open to question. This must certainly constitute a grave problem for the theologian if he takes the view that the New Testament documents constitute the definitive resource for his constructive work. Thus the theologian has to face the rather unnerving possibility that at any moment some of the main planks in his argument may give way as judgements of historical probability are revised. Confronted by this situation the theologian must either turn to a higher court of appeal for the reversal of these historical judgements (if such is to be found), or he must indeed be prepared continually to submit to revision the theological conclusions where these are based on historical material. Obviously it is exceedingly difficult and demanding for the theologian to operate rigorously and honestly in this respect. But if this is truly required, then the fascinating question must be asked as to the nature and purpose of a theological enterprise that incorporates such hazards.

The same point can be made even more penetratingly if we pass on to wider issues raised by Troeltsch's undertaking. This century has been marked by a growing occupation with a new type of philosophy of history. For the most part – though there are notable exceptions – philosophers of history have been engaged in the definition and discussion of certain analytical problems connected with history, explanation, relativism, causality, objectivity, etc. They ask what we mean by an 'historical event'; in what sense it may be called unique; how the historian's standpoint influences his historical writing; how historical knowledge compares with scientific knowledge. Patrick Gardiner has pointed out that the work done in this field by philosophers familiar with analytic methods only really began in earnest after the Second World War. None the less it is surprising how very little evidence is available that theologians have been closely associated with this form of enquiry.

This gap is rather puzzling since theology has had a long record of contact with historical thinking, especially since the rise of modern historiography at the end of the eighteenth century, which was closely linked with the critique of biblical history begun by biblical scholars. Instead, during this recent period two main tendencies may be noted:

(a) a continuation, with ever more refined tools of research, of the nineteenth century's historical enquiry into the antecedents, origins and environment of biblical Christianity;
(b) a continuation of the attempt to find a sophisticated defence in support of a flight from historical questions.

Both tendencies preclude a real opening up of biblical Christianity to the challenges of fluctuating historical science. In particular, they make it difficult for the question about the transcendental dimension in biblical Christianity to be raised except in theological and philosophical categories which the theologians find congenial. Where contact does obtain between philosophy of history and theology, theology's conduct sometimes seems erratic. It has, in a number of cases, tended to take a rather off-centre line as far as philosophy of history is concerned, which is then presented as a confirmation of a theological position. For example, in different ways Norman Sykes, James M. Robinson and Rudolf Bultmann have employed Collingwood's ideas for their own purposes without asking what has to be said about Collingwood's own position.[21] This is apologetic rather than argument. I suspect that these ventures must in the end be regarded as mistaken attempts to evade the challenge which historical science levels at theology. Instead, it seems that theology must become aware of the extreme fragility of its own position where history is concerned. It must certainly ask most carefully whether it can lay the kind of weight on the historical factor which it has done heretofore. But it must also ask what the fact of the provisional character of historical science, as an ever-present partner for theology, has to say about the latter's characteristic concerns.

The problems raised by historical science seem to reinforce the necessity of beginning 'from below' in seeking to answer the question about Jesus Christ. We have as human beings to come to terms with evidence, whether in the biblical documents, in the later tradition, or in our own world, which has no built-in reliability. For Troeltsch's insistence on the interwovenness of Christian and extra-Christian material means at the outset that we cannot claim for that Christian material an absolute and final validity for all men, in all times and at all places. To do this is precisely to isolate the Christian phenomenon from its place in the 'continual connection of becoming'. It is to ignore that this phenomenon is deeply and inextricably bound up with the relativity which belongs to all historical phenomena. There are many theologians in recent times who have seen in such conclusions the demise of Christian faith and have insisted that theology cannot to this extent be governed by historical considerations. Karl Barth's theological enterprise illustrates such a standpoint, but also illustrates the problems of such a standpoint. For Barth has not really been able to show how he can justify the limitations which he places upon the use of historical methods in theology.

It seems, then, that the theologian, when he asks the question about Jesus Christ, must either take his starting point at the historical level, or he must propose another starting-point which does not ignore the restrictions imposed by historical science. In the next chapter I shall consider the work of a theologian who appears to have taken to heart the problems of historical probability and of the interwovenness of all historical material, and yet who is still able to make high claims for the action of God in Jesus Christ.

NOTES

1. T. W. Ogletree, *Christian Faith and History*, New York 1965, p. 11.
2. A. MacIntyre, *Secularization and Moral Change*, London 1967, pp. 7 f.
3. R. G. Collingwood, *The Idea of History*, Oxford 1946, p. 209.
4. F. R. Tennant, *Philosophy of the Sciences*, Cambridge 1932, pp. 99 f.
5. E. Troeltsch, *Protestantism and Progress*, London and New York 1912, p. 34.
6. A. O. Lovejoy, cited from A. Thorlby (ed.), *The Romantic Movement*, London 1966, pp. 48 f.
7. E. Troeltsch, *Gesammelte Schriften*, Vol. 3, Tübingen 1922, p. 33.
8. *Op. cit.*, p. 54.
9. E. Troeltsch, in *Encyclopedia of Religion and Ethics*, VI, p. 720.
10. O. Hintze, *Historische Zeitschrift* 135, 1927, p. 206.
11. E. Troeltsch, *Die wissenschaftliche Lage*, Tübingen 1900, pp. 5, 8.
12. E. Troeltsch, *Zeitschrift für Theologie und Kirche* VIII, 1898, p. 4.
13. *Op. cit.*, p. 7.
14. *Op. cit.*, p. 6.
15. E. Troeltsch, *Gesammelte Schriften*, Vol. 2, Tübingen 1913, pp. 729–53.
16. *Op. cit.*, p. 732.
17. *Op. cit.*, p. 734.
18. *Op. cit.*, p. 738.
19. G. Ebeling, *Word and Faith*, London 1963, pp. 24, 48.
20. H.-G. Drescher, *Zeitschrift für Theologie und Kirche* LVII, 1960, pp. 186 f.
21. See especially T. A. Roberts, *Religious Studies* I, 1966, pp. 185 ff.

3   Jesus Christ and the Demand of the 'Moment'

In this chapter I shall be concerned with some aspects of the work of the German theologian Rudolf Bultmann (born 1884). His overall position is very complex and a subject of much scholarly dispute, so I shall confine myself as far as possible to dealing only with certain themes which bear closely on how the historical question impinges on the way in which we ask the theological question about Jesus Christ. In fact, this approach will bring us close to some of the central features of Bultmann's theological enterprise. In the first place I want to indicate Bultmann's views about the trustworthiness of the Gospel tradition, since this links up with the discussion of historical probability in Chapter 2. Then I shall try to show how, on independent grounds, Bultmann arrives at an understanding of history which allows him to treat historical scepticism with cool disregard. Finally, I shall attempt to suggest what this means for his understanding of the question about Jesus Christ.

In 1919 the New Testament scholar Martin Dibelius published a book entitled *Die Formgeschichte des Evangeliums* (The Form-History of the Gospel),[1] in which he traced the pre-literary stage of the gospel material and sought to reconstruct the way in which it was handed down. His conclusions, in general terms, were:

1. There never was a 'purely' historical witness to Jesus. Whatever was told of Jesus' words and deeds was always a test of faith as formulated for teaching and exhortation;

2. With some exceptions, our records refuse an answer

if we enquire into them about the character, the 'personality' or the qualities of Jesus;

3. Consequently, it should not be asked whether this or that was possible or actually happened, but rather how, since, when and to what end and in what sense this or that was handed down.[2]

Now Bultmann embarked, in *The History of the Synoptic Tradition* and other writings, upon a programme similar to that of Dibelius, but with a much clearer intention to use the method, 'form criticism', as a means of critically discriminating between primitive tradition and the later work of redaction. His conclusion was that the tradition provides us with a good picture of the primitive community into which the spirit of Jesus breathes. It is, moreover, possible to form a picture of Jesus as a lawgiver and prophet. On the other hand:

> the outline of the gospels does not enable us to know either the outer course of the life of Jesus or his inner development ... We can neither write 'a life of Jesus' nor present an accurate picture of his personality.[3]

There has been considerable dispute in the world of theology about this thesis since it was first presented. This is not surprising, since we can expect a wide variety of judgements as to what is, and what is not, redaction. There is also the problem as to the way in which form criticism is related to other styles of gospel criticism. The main outline of the position can be accepted, however, namely that, in John Knox's words:

> What we have in the New Testament is a record and reflection of the life and thought of the early church. This is as true of the Gospels as of the Epistles. What confronts us immediately and directly in the New Testament documents is simply and only the primitive community – what it remembered, what it knew, what it thought, what it felt.[4]

This does not, however, of itself commit us to a theory of thoroughgoing scepticism. It may be, for example, that the community remembered very accurately the things which concerned Jesus. On the other hand, it reminds us very forcibly that in the nature of the case we can only reach judgements of probability about these things. Moreover, we can expect to encounter very great difficulties in discriminating, if we wish to do so, between what was truly and actually remembered about Jesus by the early community and what was their own theological embroidery on their remembrance of things past. This is, of course, only one particular instance of the perennial problem about fact and interpretation. I do not want here to enter into a discussion of this problem, but only to note that it intensifies the fragile character of the theological undertaking.

What is more worthy of note in Bultmann's case is the fact that in his view the only recoverable elements from the history of Jesus are thoroughly human in character. On the other hand we must observe that Bultmann is not in fact out to claim that nothing can be said. We can speak of a concrete figure of history – Jesus of Nazareth, whose father and mother were well known; of the historical event of the crucifixion, and of the meaning of the historical figure of Jesus and of the events of his life.[5] We can speak of Jesus as the prophet and law-giver. But it is obvious that information of this kind does not enable us to make such statements as 'who for us men and for our salvation came down from heaven'. In other words, Bultmann in his own way takes up Troeltsch's thesis that we cannot get on to the 'supernatural' by historical means. Indeed Bultmann can deny, on form-critical grounds and (as we shall see) for other reasons too, that:

> historical research can ever encounter any traces of the epiphany of God in Christ . . . all it can do is to present us with the Jesus of history.[6]

Of course, Bultmann stands sufficiently far removed from theological liberalism to hold that this can constitute a gospel to be preached. For the Gospel concerns God's actions in Jesus Christ. But how are we to get on to this

Gospel, if not through historical science, and what might be the character of God's action witnessed to in any such Gospel?

Bultmann approaches this question in a twofold manner, part negative and part positive. Negatively he seeks to discredit the idea that, whatever historical science may or may not say, the divine action in Christ is manifested palpably in historical events. Such talk is mythological in character, that is to say it uses imagery 'to express the otherworldly in terms of this world and the divine in terms of human life, the other side in terms of this side'.[7] This is a mistaken enterprise in that the images of sense are used to describe the spiritual reality of God and in doing so distort its character. It is therefore obvious that Bultmann brings to this discussion, independently, a certain understanding about the nature of God and of his action.

It is too complex a matter at this stage to analyse the various sources for Bultmann's understanding of God and his characteristic activity. Certainly part of his appeal in this respect is to Heidegger's existential analysis of human existence. But Bultmann is also much more indebted to Luther than many commentators have allowed. The main point to observe, however, is that Bultmann regards God as a transcendent subject, personal in character, who is personally related to human subjects in their own subjectivity. The action of such a God must, according to Bultmann, fulfil certain requirements. His action must be seen as a personal encounter with man. For this encounter to remain the work of a transcendent God it must be hidden; it cannot be observed. In turn, this means that such an act cannot be, and must not be, supportable by any appeal to objective evidence. Thus God's action may not be 'read off' from an historical event.

But if God does not act towards man in observable history, where then does he act? Bultmann's answer is clear. God acts upon and within man's subjectivity, his existence. Of course, our existence is expressed to no small extent in observable events. For Bultmann this constitutes no problem. A historical event, the subject matter of historical science, may or may not also be God's action. And we have no means of knowing, from the external inspection of that event, whether it is or not. The divine action, if it is present, is hidden. The event seen from the standpoint of historical science is *historical* in the ordinary sense of the word; the event seen from the standpoint of God's action is variously described by Bultmann with the adjectives *eschatological, existential,* or *historic (geschichtlich).* There is therefore no difficulty in saying that an event can be both historical and eschatological. It is, however, the latter component which is significant for Christian theology, since it speaks of God personally acting out his personal relationship to man's subjectivity, calling it into question and asking it to understand itself anew.

In the light of these remarks it is possible to say something more directly about Bultmann's handling of the question concerning Jesus Christ. For the reasons already mentioned, we cannot point to anything about Jesus' career or personality which indicates that he is God's Word. We can, however, say that the visible, historical, acting Jesus (of whom we have some traces in the Gospel tradition) is, paradoxically, at one and the same time the one through whom God acts decisively and uniquely for men. 'The eschatological emissary of God is a concrete figure of a particular historical past.'[8] Bultmann is therefore manifestly not open to the criticism which has often been made of him, namely that he detaches the Christian proclamation from historical moorings. Thus Bultmann writes:

I stress emphatically the paradox that the eschatological event which has occurred in Jesus Christ is at the same time an historical event. I never intended to cut loose faith from history or to reduce the historical event to the existential life of man.[9]

At the same time, it must be admitted that the acts and words of Jesus' life, insofar as they can be known, are not in any particularly close relationship with God's hidden and decisive act which can confront us in Jesus. Thus Bultmann is, for example, not really troubled as to whether Jesus' teaching is particularly novel in character. For his teaching falls within the realm of historical entities which share the relativity of all history and cannot lay claim to any absolute validity. Once again it becomes apparent why Bultmann need really have no fear at all about the results of historical critical studies.

It is therefore clear, according to Bultmann, that we cannot expect to proceed very far in handling the question about Jesus Christ if we confine ourselves to historical and physical categories. Instead, we must ask what can be said about Jesus Christ if through him we are confronted in our selfhood by God's own transcendent and hidden selfhood. To begin to answer this question we must explore this idea of selfhood and its relationship to history.

Bultmann is in the first place dependent upon Heidegger's distinction between the sphere of personal, human being (*Dasein*) and the sphere of impersonal non-human being (*Vorhandenheit*). In Bultmann's view, our relationship with God, his relationship with us, and our understanding of ourselves as persons all belong to the former sphere. From the outset therefore, *both* in talking about Jesus *and* in talking about ourselves, *and* in talking about the divine action, there is no reference whatsoever to things which inhabit the objective world, e.g. human bodies. Now Heidegger makes a further, not dissimilar, distinction in talking about history. There are in effect two kinds of history. There is *Historie* which refers to things that happen in the world, i.e. history as an object of historical science, and, on the other hand, *Geschichte*, which refers to the subjective, personal and human form of existence. Bultmann draws similar distinctions, though he sometimes uses the word *Geschichte* where he means *Historie*. Be that as it may, Bultmann speaks on the one hand of 'an immanent world-

51

historical process' or of 'earthly, historical *Dasein*'. This is history as Troeltsch described it with its own internal causality. But then, on the other hand, Bultmann uses *Geschichte*, very much in Heidegger's sense, to talk about the basic constitution of our human existence. The contrast comes out in the following quotation:

> ... *Geschichte* is no neutral orientation about objectively determined past events, but is motivated by the question how we ourselves, standing in the current of history, can succeed in comprehending our own existence, can gain clear insight into the contingencies and necessities of our own life purpose.[10]

This means that as far as Christian faith and theology are concerned, the history that matters is not world-history, nor the history of Israel, nor the history of the church, nor the history of other peoples, but rather the history which each individual experiences for himself and in himself. It is in relation to this sphere that we may talk of God's action, of Jesus Christ as God's emissary, of sin and of salvation. In this sphere a man has two alternatives. Either, he can live a life of inauthentic existence, in bondage to the past, fearful of the future, imprisoned in this-worldly securities, subject to the authority of the world, treating his human life as an assured possession. This is 'life according to the flesh'. Or, he can live a life of authentic existence, based on an unseen, intangible reality which confronts men as love, a life where the forgiveness of sins is at work, where man is delivered from the bondage of the past, where he may open himself to the future, where he can live in freedom. This is the life of faith, life after the Spirit. Of course, precisely because personal life is not an assured possession, the individual does not once and for all commit himself to the life of faith, to authentic existence, and ever after live in it. Life in faith involves the imperative 'be' rather than the indicative 'I am'. As Bultmann puts it:

> The decision of faith is never final, it needs constant renewal in every fresh situation.[11]

It is important to notice that on Bultmann's view there is nothing mysterious or arcane about authentic existence. Its characteristic quality does not have to be revealed to us. It is, in fact, outlined in St Paul and St John, but it is also to be found in Heidegger. The answer which human life and thought is unable to provide concerns *the way* we are to achieve this authentic existence, *how* we are to enter upon this life of faith. Bultmann is at this point unequivocal and uncompromising. Only in an encounter with God through Jesus Christ can this possibility of authentic existence become an actuality. If, then, we are to achieve this authentic existence, we must somehow encounter Jesus Christ who is both an historical figure whose mother and father are known, and who is at the same time the one through whom (and through whom alone) God acts in a hidden way presenting man with the opportunity to realise authentic existence:

Bultmann has always maintained that the real possibility of man's actualizing his true life is entirely dependent on the historical event of Jesus of Nazareth, in which God's gracious judgement is uniquely actualized.[12]

We are then faced by the further question as to how a contemporary man is to come into contact with Jesus Christ, granted that Jesus Christ is not available to us, in any way that matters, by a process of historical reconstruction. Bultmann is not troubled by this difficulty since he holds that the encounter with Jesus Christ takes place *in the present*, through the preaching of the church. When I hear and obey the challenge contained in the preaching, I find myself part of that original event in which God acted hiddenly in the historical person of Jesus. Bultmann seems to suggest that this original eschatological event is not tied to the same kind of chronology as ordinary historical events. For he writes that:

the eschatological event that has its origin in Jesus Christ continues to fulfil itself as eschatological event in the preaching of the Church and in faith which responds to that preaching.

Indeed, the contemporary man cannot get on to God's act in any other way, for:

> Jesus Christ is the eschatological event not as an established fact of past time but as repeatedly present, as addressing you and me here and now in the preaching.[13]

These and other areas of Bultmann's thought need to be, and have been, discussed in much greater detail than is possible here. From this discussion I want, however, to pick on one main point which is crucial for our discussion of the question concerning Jesus Christ, Bultmann's answer to the question *how* we enter upon genuine historical existence. He insists, as we have seen, that this is only possible because God has acted in Christ.

> Thus eschatological existence has become possible. God has acted . . The New Testament speaks and faith knows of an act of God through which man becomes capable of self-commitment, capable of faith and love, of his authentic life.[14]

Bultmann quite explicitly rejects the accusation that he speaks of authentic existence being achieved by reflection on Jesus Christ, and by my then bringing about, out of my own resources, a change in my self-understanding. He speaks rather of 'God's action which cannot be directed by man, but which reaches man as an event from beyond himself'.[15]

Yet in some sense it appears that at this point Bultmann is proving inconsistent in his overall argument. He appears to be doing violence to his own concept of myth, for we might expect that 'God's decisive *action* in Christ' would be dispatched along with the other mythical imagery of the New Testament. Is not this precisely to talk of a transcendent and hidden God in terms of this world? Does not Bultmann also at this one point compromise that understanding of history which Troeltsch exemplified and by virtue of which we may not reasonably interrupt the lateral interrelatedness of history with vertical divine descents, however hidden they may be? On the other hand, if Bultmann had wished to surrender all talk of God's decisive action in Christ, would he not in fact have surrendered the one thing that characteristically Christians want to affirm about Jesus Christ? This is very perplexing.

On the one hand, Bultmann wishes, it appears, to remain faithful to the traditional Christian assertion that 'God was in Christ reconciling the world to himself'. He also wishes to remain faithful to the idea which belongs to much, but not all, of traditional Christianity, that salvation occurs through Christ and through Christ alone. On the other hand, by his remarkable account of human selfhood, he has responded admirably to the historical critique of theology by insisting that the locus and means of God's action towards men must be firmly integrated within our personal experience of the reality in which we are set. By this insistence Bultmann finally shakes off the notion of a salvation history parallel with, sometimes touching, but never truly part of, our own existence. He has thereby shaken off, too, the idea that God performs his action on behalf of men through some transaction external to men in some mysterious sphere to which men have no personal access. In this sense Bultmann appears truly to have taken to heart Troeltsch's concern that theology should take full account of the richness, profusion and interconnectedness of human historical life.

Bultmann has in fact been at some pains to reply to the charge that this talk of God's action is mythological in character, and to this I shall refer before going on to summarize and comment on the content of this chapter. Bultmann wants to remind his critics that in speaking of God's action he is not speaking, as theology sometimes has done, of an intervention in the natural or historical course of events. To do this would be for him to put the transcendent God on the level of other entities. God's action is rather one which happens *within* events which have their own proper causal network. This action, which is hidden, can only be discerned by faith; to the secular eye it is quite invisible. It operates at the level of our personal existence. Thus 'God as acting' does not refer to an event which can be perceived by me without myself being drawn into the event as into God's action, without myself taking part in it as being acted upon. In other words, 'to speak of God as acting involves the events of personal existence'.[16] It is for this reason that Bultmann describes 'God's action' as analogical rather than mythical talk. God's action may be described by analogy with actions which take place between men. To talk about a human action is not to speak of an idea about a man, it is to speak of the man himself. Similarly, to talk about God's action is not to put forward an idea about him but to speak of him directly as people who have experience of him. Thus Bultmann returns to the point made earlier, that we may only make statements about God if they refer to an existential relationship between God and man. Statements of any other kind are mythological in character and may not be allowed. To talk of God as acting is to talk of a relationship between a personal being and persons. As such it is admissible and indeed entirely appropriate.

If we accept the need for theology to retain the priority of God's action as the condition for man achieving salvation, then it is clearly necessary to hold on in some way or another to the notion of God's action. Whether Bultmann's particular defence of such talk is adequate is another matter. To that question I shall return in the next chapter. But granted for the present Bultmann's argument, it does not seem to follow that God's action must be *confined* to the eschatological event of Jesus Christ and to the re-presentations of that event when the Christ is preached. This is a point of considerable significance in our asking of the question about Jesus Christ. Is he the one in whom alone God's decisive and unique action for man's salvation occurs? With some qualifications Bultmann seems to answer this question in the affirmative. Christian belief:

asserts indeed that man apart from Christianity could not arrive at an answer (about God) ... It asserts that all *answers* apart from the Christian answer are *illusions*.[17]

We have already noted that Bultmann does not require that the description of authentic existence should emanate from Christ alone or from Christianity alone. Non-Christian descriptions are quite in order, since 'there is nothing mysterious or supernatural about the Christian life'. Indeed Bultmann can just about say that there is revelation in other religions. That non-Christians ask questions about God and propose answers is a sign of this revelation:

> Now I do not deny that there is an understanding outside of Christian faith as to what God is and what grace is.[18]

But Bultmann is clearly uneasy about this. He takes the view that it is a very different thing to encounter Christ in the preaching, to have faith in him and to realize authentic existence. All this, strictly speaking, is dependent upon the one action of God in Jesus Christ. Unlike Troeltsch, Bultmann believes that at this point it is possible to concentrate the absolute in one place, though this concentration occurs *within* history without being *part* of it. Troeltsch, on the other hand, writes:

> To desire the absolute in history, in an absolute way and at an individual point, is an illusion which collapses not only by virtue of the fact that it cannot be shown to be the case, but also because such a desire would be an inner contradiction of the nature of all historical religion.[19]

Bultmann in turn would, however, insist that the absolute *is* so present, and would applaud the fact that this cannot be shown to be the case! If it *could* be shown to be the case, the notions of faith and of God's hidden and transcendent personal being would fall in ruins:

> The man who wants to believe in God as his God, must realize that he comes with his hands empty of anything in which he might believe,

57

that he is, as it were, suspended in mid-air, being able to demand no proof for the truth of the word which addresses him.[20]

While Bultmann's position must be respected, the question cannot be left there. In the next chapter I shall want to ask what is involved for theology and for our understanding of Jesus Christ if this exclusive claim for Jesus Christ is withdrawn.

I want now to make some general observations about the kind of model or pattern which Bultmann has employed for his talk about Jesus Christ. The first thing to be said is that he has met the challenge of historical science, but at some serious cost. Bultmann's scheme can allow for almost any judgement of historical probability to be reached about Jesus Christ. That Bultmann does not commit himself to any such arbitrariness is more a reflection upon his scholarly skill than a consequence of his theoretical position. But in fact this immunity of theology from historical research turns Troeltsch upon his head. For Troeltsch emphasized precisely the opposite, namely, the need for theology to accept a far greater involvement in the vagaries and the richness of historical science. Bultmann, on the other hand, appears to see little organic connection between Jesus as God's eschatological emissary and the history which surrounds him, though he can, of course, assert full historical causality at the level of the historical Jesus as prophet and law-giver. This results in a strange impoverishment of the available historical resources, not least in the virtual exclusion of the Old Testament except as a comment on man's failure to attain to God, and as a general preparations for a Christian understanding of existence. In other words, the total cultural-historical setting of Jesus is virtually ignored at the theological level, though it is skilfully and imaginatively penetrated by Bultmann at the level of his historical researches.

This difficulty is only an instance of a much wider problem

presented by Bultmann's thought. This can best be expressed by drawing attention to the dualistic streak which runs through all his writings. This dualism emerges in a variety of ways. The following are common examples: nature/history; objective history/personal history; object/subject; cosmology/anthropology. Again and again Bultmann insists on treating these and other pairs as alternatives:

> *either* the proposition of the divinity of Christ is interpreted cosmologically and 'objectifyingly' *or* it is interpreted soteriologically and 'existentially'. *Tertium non datur!*[21]

It has been pointed out that an insistence on such dualism plays havoc with New Testament exegesis; it also plays havoc, I would suggest, with the general understanding which we have of the world.

A similar problem arises from Bultmann's treatment of history. The only history with which he is concerned, from a theological point of view, is personal history. But surely man does, and must, reach out for a far wider view of things than this – a reaching out which finds full expression in the Bible:

> Whoever structures history, and so bears responsibility for the future, in my opinion must believe in a meaning in history, a meaning which is realized not only in the individual moment, but also in the course of history. And this meaning must in every moment appear as the meaning of history as a whole, since, as is the case today, we are gaining a world-wide view which encompasses all mankind.[22]

It has been said that Bultmann is not himself entirely satisfied with the narrower view. This may be so. But at the same time he can be quoted to the following effect:

> In any case . . . the kingdom of God has nothing to do with civilization. . . . Man is not asked about the significance of being, the significance of history and civilization. . . . Man is asked, as it appears to me, only about the significance of the 'moment', and that means about the demand of the 'moment'.[23]

Finally, this dualism comes to rest in the person of Christ. There appear to be very few lines of connection between the historical Jesus and the eschatological emissary of God. If I understand him aright, Bultmann would indeed expect that we should find no such lines of connection since it is a paradoxical event. The way Bultmann presents this, namely that the particular human identity of Jesus has hardly any bearing upon God's action in him, seems to smack of a division between the two natures of Christ which the fifth-century Fathers of the church were unwilling to accept as orthodox. This same difficulty is reflected in Bultmann's understanding of personal existence. This personal existence does not appear to be firmly rooted in man's bodily life. It does not appear to take sufficiently into account the extent to which man is made what he is by his heredity and his environment, nor the extent to which he is unable to escape being what he is on account of these and other factors. Bultmann's picture thus represents a somewhat limited and one-sided view of the situation.

Difficulties of a not dissimilar kind also arise in his treatment of 'faith' and 'knowledge'. There seems to be considerable alarm on Bultmann's part lest, in saying in a theological context that we know or want to know something, we thereby undermine faith. But there are a number of themes which the Bible and Christian theology have subjected to discussion, e.g. death, which cannot be treated without reference to natural or other empirical phenomena. Death does affect love and joy and peace, but it also affects our bodies. It therefore seems entirely proper that our faith in God's final victory over death should include enquiries and knowledge about physical death. In practice this seems to enhance rather than to undermine faith, since the more we learn about the physical constitution and fate of our bodies, the more remarkable must faith find God's promise to be in respect of a victory over death!

In Chapter 1, I referred to the need, if we are comprehensively to ask the question about Jesus Christ 'from below', to attend with equal comprehensiveness to evidence of a threefold kind, to the historical evidence about Jesus, to the evidence of the later theological tradition, and to the evidence contained in the understanding we have of the world. It seems that Bultmann by virtue of his over-reaction to the historical problem, by virtue of his dualism (whose roots in Luther, Kant, Heidegger and others I shall not begin to explore here) has too narrowly confined the scope of our attention towards this three-pronged evidence. By so doing he can in one sense be said to have rescued Jesus Christ from a full-blooded insertion into the relativities of history, and thus to have maintained intact the claim that in Jesus is the unique and exclusive action of God for man's salvation is found. But if we think on other grounds that the price which Bultmann has paid for this rescue operation is too high, we are bound to reconsider the validity of these claims. In doing so we have to reckon with the possibility that in the end we shall be able to make claims so tentative that we cast serious doubt upon most of the traditional Christian affirmations about Jesus Christ. But we also have to keep as a live option the possibility that, if we are willing to attend to the evidence in a more comprehensive way, we might discover that the Christian claims can be worked out in a way which not only respects our understanding of the world, but enhances and even corrects it.

In the next chapter I want to take up this possibility in one direction, namely an exploration of what might be involved if we withdraw from Bultmann's account of the insistence on Jesus Christ as the exclusive and unique divine action of God towards men. In adopting this course, and notwithstanding the criticisms I have levelled at Bultmann, I take the stand that Bultmann's account of personal existence within the reality in which we are set as the primary locus of the divine action cannot be gainsaid. It remains to be seen whether that insight can be developed in a way which is most faithful to the historical question and to the threefold evidence mentioned above. The extent to which a developed view of personal existence can be supplemented and enriched in other ways will be discussed in later chapters. In this way we in fact begin to clarify the character of the question which we ask about Jesus Christ, although, as I indicated in my first chapter, I do not (in the nature of things) necessarily expect any dramatic or definitive answer to this question.

NOTES

1. Tübingen 1919.

2. M. Dibelius, *Theologische Rundschau*, NF 1, 1929, p. 10.

3. R. Bultmann, *Existence and Faith* (ed. Schubert M. Ogden), London 1961, p.52.

4. John Knox, *The Church and the Reality of Christ*, London 1963, p. 9.

5. H.-W. Bartsch (ed.), *Kerygma and Myth*, London 1957, pp. 34 f., 37, 134.

6. *Op. cit.*, pp. 117 f.

7. *Op. cit.*, p. 10, n. 2.

8. *Op. cit.*, p. 43.

9. C. W. Kegley (ed.), *The Theology of Rudolf Bultmann*, London 1966, p. 278.

10. R. Bultmann, *Jesus and the Word*, London 1934, p. 10.

11. *Kerygma and Myth*, p. 21.

12. *The Theology of Rudolf Bultmann*, p. 121.

13. *Op. cit.*, pp. 276 f.

14. *Kerygma and Myth*, pp. 32 f.

15. *The Theology of Rudolf Bultmann*, p. 262.

16. R. Bultmann, *Jesus Christ and Mythology*, London 1960, p. 68.

17. R. Bultmann, *Essays Philosophical and Theological*, London 1955, p. 98.

18. *The Theology of Rudolf Bultmann*, p. 275.

19. E. Troeltsch, *Die Absolutheit des Christentums*, second edition, Tübingen 1912, p. 98.

20. H.-W. Bartsch (ed.), *Kerygma und Mythos*, Vol. 2, Hamburg 1952, p. 207.

21. H. Ott, *Geschichte und Heilsgeschichte*, Tübingen 1955, p. 50.

22. Criticism by Ott, in: *The Theology of Rudolf Bultmann*, p. 63.

23. R. Bultmann, *Essays*, p. 289.

4 The Decisive Manifestation of Divine Love

In this chapter I seek to begin to ask the question whether we are not required to detach the notion of 'realizing authentic existence' from the notion of a 'unique action of God in Jesus Christ'. I want to consider whether this is not required on both negative and positive grounds – negative, because the combination of the two runs counter to our understanding of history; and positive, because the combination imposes unfortunate restrictions upon our understanding of the relationship of God to the world. I shall illustrate my discussion by reference to the work of two theologians who have responded critically, at this one crucial point, to Bultmann's theological enterprise. These are the Basel theologian Fritz Buri and the American scholar Schubert Ogden.

Buri[1] is extremely sympathetic to Bultmann's concern to rid Christian theology of its mythical elements and to understand these afresh as statements about the personal, existential relationship of God, as a personal being, to human and personal beings. On this view, theological statements do not refer to some supposedly objective actions which happen in the world, but rather to events between God and man which go in the understanding which a person has of himself. While Buri applauds this point of view, he finds it difficult to understand why Bultmann should insist on retaining the notion of an act of divine salvation which has happened once and for all in Jesus Christ. Is not this a reversion to the mythology which Bultmann has rejected?

Buri is not concerned with this supposed remnant of mythology for its own sake, but also for the implication which it bears in respect of the way we understand the human condition. Presumably, if Bultmann believed that man was capable of realizing his true existence, he would have no need for the kind of divine action which in fact he retains. Buri correctly observes how Bultmann's insistence that man is in fact *in*capable of realizing his authentic existence is a product of his understanding of *sin*. Sin has effected a radical gulf between man's profane and inauthentic existence and his need for authentic existence. This gulf can only be bridged if God operates, as it were from without, to make possible the overcoming of this profane existence. But according to Buri, such a view of sin as a permanent endowment or natural condition in man is itself hopelessly mythological in character. It is, Buri continues, totally out of character with Bultmann's otherwise impressive account of the personal and historical character of human existence.

Buri has certainly drawn attention to a problematical and perhaps inconsistent feature of Bultmann's theological scheme. For in more than one place Bultmann goes to some trouble to insist that, when we talk about personal existence, we do not have in mind any theory of 'substantial nature' (Gk. *physis*). He regards 'personality', not as a fixed or static concept, but rather as the changing centre-point of an individual's decisions. It is something which is always in the process of becoming and is therefore 'constant only as a possibility which is ever to be realized'.[2] Given this account of personal existence, we have to ask why it must be that man is incapable of realizing his authentic existence if the possibility for doing it is presented to him. Obviously there will be many occasions and situations when man in fact fails to realize the life of faith. But this does not of itself mean that he is incapable of doing so. It seems, on the other hand, as if Bultmann is suggesting that beneath and within the self at the level of actions, there is some kind of flaw which makes man impotent to realize his authentic existence.

Ogden puts a similar question to Bultmann in the following way. According to Ogden,[3] Bultmann's argument may be summarized under two headings.

1. We may say that Christian faith is to be interpreted exhaustively as referring to man's original possibility of authentic existence. What is involved in this authentic existence can be clarified and put into concepts by the kind of philosophical analysis which Heidegger and others have undertaken. (This repeats the point which I made in the last chapter that for Bultmann there is nothing supernatural or mysterious about the Christian life.)

2. Christian faith is *actually realizable* only because of the particular historical event of Jesus Christ as Bultmann has described this.

Now Ogden insists (as does Buri) that, as they stand, these two propositions are incompatible. Which, then, shall give way to the other? Ogden takes the view that the first proposition is an entirely proper account of what the New Testament, underneath its misleading mythology, is saying. The two propositions are incompatible since, if we really agree to interpret Christian faith in terms of man's understanding of his personal existence, we cannot then tie Christian faith to any one particular historical occurrence which stands apart from that existence. It is therefore the second proposition which must be modified or rejected.

Ogden seems, however, to be aware of Bultmann's motive in holding on (however inconsistently) to the necessary connection of Christian faith with a particular historical event. He recognizes that Bultmann wishes to avoid saying that we enter upon authentic existence simply by deciding to do so. We must truly be presented with the possibility of doing so by the action of God towards us, and this 'action' must be other than, and prior to, us; it must be more than a self-generated change in our understanding. Ogden asks, therefore, whether it is possible to retain this proper objectivity of God's action towards us, while at the same time not tying that action to a single and exclusive historical event. Ogden holds that this is possible, namely that we can *both* retain the understanding of Christian faith in terms of personal existence, *and* speak meaningfully of God's objective action towards us, *and* avoid the perils of subjectivism.

According to Ogden, we can steer between Scylla and Charybdis by examining with care what it might mean to talk of God's objective action *within* the framework of Christian faith understood in terms of personal existence. In other words, we must seek to discern and to elucidate both a subjective and an objective reference *within* the existential account of authentic existence which Bultmann develops. Ogden further holds that the most useful resource available to us for such an enterprise lies with 'process philosophy'.[4] Using this framework, it is possible truly to speak of a 'God-who-is-turned-towards-man' without lapsing into myth. But 'turning', as this style of thought expounds it, involves a qualification of the idea that God is turned to man exclusively in Jesus Christ, as it involves too a very different account of the character of God's 'action'. I will deal with these two points in turn.

One of the premises of the philosophical position which Ogden brings to the problem of exclusivity is, as I have already hinted, the idea that we only get on to notions such as 'God' and 'reality' by analysing our experiences as human subjects and by then using our imagination to draw up generalizations on the basis of these experiences. Thus, if we say that the being of the self is relational, social and involved in processive change, we shall at the end of the day assert that God, too, must be conceived of as a truly temporal and social reality. He is, of course, *the* eminently temporal and social reality since he is, as God, in all ways supreme and qualitatively different from everything else. I shall not develop the argument as it leads from these assertions to the view that this God is eternal, unchangeable and absolute. It is the other pole of this 'bi-polar' thesis which concerns us here, namely that as the eminently relative, temporal and social reality God is related to the universe of others in a real, immediate and direct way. Consequently, when this understanding of God's turning to, and relationship with, all others is set fully in the context of the Christian affirmation of God as pure unbounded love, we cannot postulate only one event in which the turning of that loving God is uniquely and exclusively located. When God is understood in this way, we have to allow that every man in every place and at every time has to be seen as a 'man-who-comes-from-God' and as a 'man-to-whom-God-is-turned'. This means that, in whatever way we are to understand Jesus Christ, we cannot understand him as contradicting this insight.

Ogden suggests that such a point of view does not stand without witnesses in the New Testament tradition. Moreover, with such a point of view we are enabled to adopt a more positive estimate of the Old Testament tradition than, for example, Bultmann can countenance. Thus:

> ... it would never have occurred to Paul to doubt that the righteousness of God revealed in Jesus of Nazareth had already been attested by God's dealing with Israel and thence, as he says, through 'the law and the prophets'.[5]

Naturally we cannot turn to the New Testament to clinch the argument. At the weakest, however, it is certainly possible to say that there is little in the Scriptural witness which is positively repugnant to this point of view, though the same cannot be said of certain moments in the ensuing tradition.

I shall now cite five statements from Ogden which together express with some precision the consequences which follow from this estimate of Jesus Christ:

> 1. The church stands by the claim that the decisive manifestation of this divine word is none other than the human word of Jesus of Nazareth. . . . But the point of this claim is not that the Christ is manifest only in Jesus and nowhere else, but that the word addressed

to men *everywhere*, in all the events of their lives, is none other than the word spoken in Jesus and in the preaching and sacraments of the church.[6]

2. Christian faith is always a 'possibility in fact' because of the unconditional gift and demand of God's love, which is the ever-present ground and end of all created things; the decisive manifestation of this divine love, however, is the event Jesus of Nazareth, which fulfils and corrects all other manifestations.[7]

3. The New Testament claim 'only in Jesus Christ' must be interpreted to mean not that God acts to redeem only in the event of Jesus and in no other event, but that the only God who acts to redeem any event – *although he in fact redeems every event* – is the God whose redemptive action is decisively revealed in the word that Jesus speaks and is.[8]

4. Men can realize their true life as men, and thus enjoy essential salvation, only if they understand themselves in the way concretely re-presented to them in Jesus' word and deed and tragic destiny.[9]

5. The New Testament sense of the claim 'only in Jesus Christ' is not that God is only to be found in Jesus and nowhere else but that the only God who is to be found anywhere – *though he is to be found everywhere* – is the God who is made known in the word that Jesus speaks and is.[10]

I now go on to the second aspect of Ogden's critique of Bultmann, namely the problem of God's action. We observe that in these five quoted statements, Ogden uses such phrases as 'God acts' and 'God redeems'. How does Ogden intend this language? We have already noted, in a preliminary way, that this language is neither objective language of the kind which Bultmann rejects as myth, nor subjective in that it only refers to self-reflection. But what precise meaning does Ogden want to convey between these two extremes? Ogden in fact deals with this question at length in an essay entitled 'What Sense Does It Make To Say "God Acts in History"?'.[11] This is a rich and carefully argued piece of work from which I can only extract what seem to me the most relevant themes. I have already mentioned that Ogden believes he can find within a philosophy of existence an objective reference which might be used for talking *about* God; that he regards this factor as dormant in Bultmann's scheme of things; but that it can be elicited and given due weight with the help of process philosophy. Bultmann, it may be noted, is not impressed by this proposal: 'I do not consider such a philosophical theology possible'.[12] In a way that is characteristic of this philosophy, Ogden takes as his starting-point our experience, as human beings, of our own actions. He then goes on to expound the meaning of God's action by strict analogy with our own. I shall omit his discussion of how we may speak of God acting upon himself, and confine my remarks to his treatment of the way that God may be said to act in history.

Ogden has two classes of action in mind. In the first place we may think of all our bodily actions as to some extent our actions as selves. So by analogy with the relation of ourselves to our bodies, we may say that every creature is to some extent God's act. But more important for our purposes is the way in which Ogden understands the second class of actions. By virtue of the fact that we are self-conscious creatures, who can understand ourselves and others, there are *some* of our actions which are peculiarly ours (in the way that *all* our actions are not), especially those which concern our relationships with others:

> This is particularly true of those distinctively human actions in which, through word and deed, we give symbolic expression to our own inner beings and understandings.[13]

Ogden refers, for example, to the way in which he comes to a fuller understanding of his wife, and thus of himself, too, through certain very particular words and deeds which she directs towards him. These words and deeds are hers in a very special sense since they express her inner attitude towards him in a way which does not happen through all her words and deeds. By analogy with this, Ogden argues that when we say of a particular creaturely happening in history that it characteristically expresses God's action as Creator and Redeemer, we may truly speak of it as God's action in a special sense. Thus the creaturely happening may be said in some sense to symbolize God's action. (Of course this expressing or symbolizing of God's action may be partial or distorted.) Now while all sorts of creaturely happenings may serve to express or symbolize God's characteristic action as Creator and Reedemer, we have seen that Ogden prefers to lay stress upon human words and deeds as being uniquely suited to perform this function. Through them above all we may speak of God's transcendent action being re-presented in such a way that we may call them God's acts.

It is now possible, in the light of this discussion of God's actions, to see how Ogden comes to formulate an understanding of Jesus Christ. He starts, as must be made clear, with the avowed premise that, like any other Christian theologian, he naturally assumes Jesus Christ to be the decisive act of God. The question is then as to the sense in which Jesus Christ is to be regarded as the decisive act of God. We have already seen that Jesus Christ is not the only act of God. God acts, in the way described above, in all events. He acts pre-eminently in human words and deeds. But none of these 'acts', these expressions of God's characteristic action as Creator and Redeemer, are necessarily complete. In the case of Jesus Christ, however, his words and deeds as the re-presentation of God's characteristic and all-embracing action and love are complete and decisive. They can therefore 'fulfil' and 'correct' all other manifestations. Jesus Christ is 'a definitive re-presentation of man's existence before God'. He is the 'final reality of God's love that confronts us as sovereign gift and demand in all the events of our existence'.[14]

These, and other similar quotations, do not, however, take us any further in specifying what it is about Jesus which enables us to accept the claim of his decisiveness. In response to this Ogden writes:

To say with the Christian community, then, that *Jesus* is the decisive act of God is to say that in him, in his outer acts of symbolic word and deed, there is expressed *that* understanding of human existence which is, in fact, the ultimate truth about our life before God.[15]

This is a very interesting statement, inasmuch as it throws us back upon the historical Jesus in a way that Bultmann's thesis did not. Bultmann could not appeal to Jesus' words and deeds in the same way lest the impression might be given that God's act in Jesus was supportable – let alone demonstrable – by objective evidence.

Ogden is, however, unequivocal in this respect. Jesus' preaching, healing, his fellowship with sinners and his death, express symbolically an understanding of existence understood in terms of God as pure unbounded love, in surrender to which we realize authentic existence. We have in consequence to ask the question – sharply posed by Troeltsch and Bultmann among others – as to whether we may on historical grounds make such claims on the basis of the New Testament evidence. Putting the issue at its sharpest, would it matter for Ogden's thesis if we came at the end of the day to the judgement that Jesus preached the opposite of what he is reported to have preached, that he did not heal, that he kept company only with aristocrats, and that he died a very different death without fortitude or compassion? The answer must surely be that these conclusions would overturn Ogden's thesis. I do not myself hold that we are ever likely to be confronted with the need to accept historical judgements such as I have just instanced. But putting the question in this extreme form does force us to ask how Ogden believes that the kind of historical judgements which he makes have sufficient reliability to assume so important a role in his argument.

At this point Ogden is, on his own confession, indebted to the theological movement called 'The New Quest of the Historical Jesus' or the 'post-Bultmannian' school, with which the names of Ernst Fuchs, Gerhard Ebeling, Ernst Käsemann and James M. Robinson are associated. Speaking in very general terms, we can say that these writers admit that it is exceedingly difficult to establish continuity between the tradition about Jesus and Jesus as a possible figure of biography. On the other hand, they claim that the tradition does in fact shed light on a different level of continuity, namely between what is preached about Jesus (and which is available in the New Testament writings) and Jesus' selfhood, his own understanding of himself. This selfhood is, moreover, adequately recoverable from an historical point of view since there is in the tradition a coherent and basically reliable witness to the *character*, if not to the details, of Jesus's actions in word and deed. While this type of approach may be acceptable at the historical level, in the sense that there are strong warrants for it in the available documents, there is a further difficulty which cannot be ignored. How secure is the link between outer symbolic actions and inner selfhood?

A colleague of Ogden's has formulated the following pertinent questions: Can one claim to know the real motives of an action? Is the thought behind the action the same thing as the motive? Must a motive be conscious? Can the historian discern motives which the actor himself is not aware of?[16] Although these questions are presumably unanswerable at the theoretical level, I do not think that this is fatal for Ogden's thesis. The person who turns to Christ's symbolic actions as God's decisive act, will (I suppose) have to discover in his own experience what resonance Jesus' outer words and deeds have for him. We have here reached the point where further verification becomes impossible; where a certain circularity afflicts (or enriches) the argument, since we take to this encounter with Jesus the fruits of God's actions upon us at all times and places of our life. Such fruitful circularity or interchange is not possible on Bultmann's scheme, since God acts to redeem in Christ alone and nowhere else. But because on Ogden's scheme Jesus Christ is the decisive, but not the exclusive, act of God, we do not approach Jesus with empty hands but with already certain authentic intimations of God's pure unbounded love.

72

I hold that Ogden has set us on the path to an understanding of Jesus Christ which is more faithful to the tradition and to our understanding of our world than Bultmann's account allows. At the same time, some of the criticisms which I raised against Bultmann must also stand against Ogden. That is to say, I still find in Ogden a streak which was a dominant feature of Bultmann's theological enterprise. This is exemplified in Ogden's decision, following Bultmann's example, to interpret Christian faith without remainder in terms of man's personal existence. I would agree with this policy with reference to what is included, but I would dissent from it in respect of what is omitted. It is unfaithful to our own understanding of the world that we should ask questions about personal existence in isolation from the many scientific, psychological, sociological and other questions which partly enrich and give a context to that personal existence, and which partly question its autonomy in theory and threaten its livedness in practice. Likewise, and (I hope) instructively, Ogden's limitation on the scope of theological statements is also unfaithful to the New Testament tradition where, unless we swallow whole Bultmann's concept of myth, the question about the identity of Jesus Christ is also asked in terms of questions about the material cosmos and the course of history. In contrast, Ogden (following F. D. Maurice) speaks of making clear that the 'hidden power, the inner meaning, the real substance, of *all* human happenings is the event of Christ'.[17] The Nicene Creed does not limit the meaning of Christ to *human* happenings alone.

I am not sure whether this is a judgement which applies to all theologies thus far derived from process philosophy, but I find here a reluctance to develop Jesus' significance beyond personal categories. If Jesus Christ is a given event which may be taken as a 'significant clue or key to the cosmic drive',[18] then I would expect that theological discourse about him would extend beyond, though it must of course comprehensively include, talk about God-man and

73

man-man relationships. There is no doubt that if we extend our discourse in this way we come upon very serious difficulties about the way we are able to relate cosmological assertions about 'Christ' to the empirical realities of the historical Jesus. I shall return to this question in a later chapter.

For the next stage of my discussion, however, I want to explore further the function and place of 'symbol' in relation to the question about Jesus Christ. This theme came to the fore towards the end of the present chapter when Ogden examined how words and deeds could re-present characteristic attitudes, both human and divine. Now Van Harvey, in a discerning essay about the contemporary theological situation, has written about his sympathy towards those 'theologies which are empirical, in the sense of continually trying to relate Christian symbols to the structures of men's actual existence'.[19] I shall try to show, from an analysis of work by Karl Jaspers and Fritz Buri, what might be one positive yield from such an approach. At the same time, and although this method seems to overcome some of the historical problems which beset us, I shall also want to ask whether the way of symbols does justice to the undoubted particular, physical and historical existence of Jesus Christ.

NOTES

1. H.-W. Bartsch (ed.), *Kerygma und Mythos*, Vol. 2, Hamburg 1952, pp. 85 ff.

2. R. Bultmann, *History and Eschatology*, Edinburgh 1957, p. 146.

3. Schubert M. Ogden, *Christ without Myth*, London 1962, p. 30.

4. Ogden, *op. cit.*, p. 179, referring to the process philosophy of Charles Hartshorne. See also Ogden's essay in: Reese and Freeman (eds.), *Process and Divinity: The Hartshorne Festschrift*, Evanston 1964, pp. 493 ff.

5. *Christ without Myth*, p. 180.

6. *Op. cit.*, p. 183.

7. *Op. cit.*, p. 179.

8. C. W. Kegley (ed.), *The Theology of Rudolf Bultmann*, London 1966, p. 122.

9. *Ibid.*

10. *Christ without Myth*, p. 168.

11. Schubert M. Ogden, *The Reality of God*, London 1967, pp. 164 ff.

12. *The Theology of Rudolf Bultmann*, p. 273.

13. *Op. cit.*, p. 181.

14. *Christ without Myth*, p. 189.

15. *The Reality of God*, pp. 185 f.

16. Van A. Harvey, *The Historian and the Believer*, London 1967, p. 191.

17. *Christ without Myth*, p. 182.

18. In this instance, Norman Pittenger in: A. Richardson (ed.), *A Dictionary of Christian Theology*, London 1969, p. 276. See also Pittenger's *Process Thought and Christian Faith*, London 1968, ch. 3.

19. Dean Peerman (ed.), *Frontline Theology*, London 1967, p. 113.

5   Reading the Cipher of Jesus

It is convenient and instructive to begin a discussion of Karl
Jaspers (1883–1969) by noting some of his criticism of
Bultmann's programme of demythologizing. Above all,
Jaspers accuses Bultmann, both as a philosopher and a
theologian, of falling prey to a false absolutism. In consequence, his work must be judged a 'most peculiar mixture
of false enlightenment and high-handed orthodoxy'.[1] This
is not one criticism among many from Jaspers. For, as I
shall show, it reflects one of the basic and controlling
features of his philosophy.

Jaspers reserves weighty criticism both for the assump-
tions behind Bultmann's programme and the results of its
execution. First, he argues, Bultmann erroneously believes
that modern science has a 'total world-view' which can be
set over against that of myth. This is a mistaken contention,
for:

> because it takes seriously the principles of cogent, universal and
> systematic knowledge, science is always aware of its limitations,
> understands the particularity of its insights, and knows that it no-
> where explores Being, but only objects in the world.[2]

To imagine that science gives final results which refer to the
totality of things is to make absolute the actual results of
science and distort them, and to promote spuriously scientific world-views. There is *no* modern scientific world-view
as such.

Secondly, and on similar lines, Bultmann is chastised by
Jaspers for seeking a 'scientific philosophy' in Heidegger.
On its own account the search for *one* scientific philosophy

is mistaken; it is even more mistaken when, as is the case with Heidegger's *Being and Time*, a very individual and experiential philosophical vision is treated as universally valid. Jaspers writes:

> The whole of this book is not motivated by the mere will to know reality as it is, but by *a* fundamental experience of human existence, not by *the* fundamental experience of human existence, in the sense of universally valid experience.[3]

Now essentially the same kind of accusation comes to the fore when Jaspers, at a later stage in the same essay, compares what he calls 'orthodoxy' and 'liberality', especially in respect of the concept of revelation. Whereas orthodoxy believes that:

> God manifests himself at a given place and time, that he has revealed himself directly at one place and time and only there and then,[4]

liberal faith recognizes that the revelation of truth is a mystery, a series of sudden illuminations in the history of the mind. Liberal faith:

> repudiates the idea of an exclusive truth formulated in a credo. ... It recognizes that the way to God is possible also without Christ, and that Asians can find it without the Bible.[5]

Underlying this argument is Jaspers' theory of 'ciphers', which I shall discuss later. Jaspers allows that Bultmann recognizes the danger of regarding myth as material, objective reality. But, faced by this danger, the task of the philosopher is not to remove myth but rather to recognize it as a code, to counter this materialist perversion and degradation of the cipher-language of myth by recovering mythical thought in its original purity and appropriating the marvellous contents of myth that deepen us morally, enlarge us as human beings and indirectly bring us closer to the idea of God which no myth can fully express.[6]

At the same time, this cipher language of myth must be seen as historically conditioned, as relative. Thus the truth which it mediates cannot lay claim to universal, absolute validity. We cannot go further into the particulars of this debate, but it is interesting to note here that Jaspers is much closer to Buri's point of view than to that of Bultmann. It is clear that there is a fundamental gulf between Bultmann and Jaspers over the question of 'absoluteness' and 'exclusiveness' in revelation. For Bultmann, in the last resort, salvation is a response to a unique revelatory eschatological act of God in Jesus Christ. Although, as we have seen, this assertion may have to be regarded as an inconsistency in his total programme, Bultmann insists that such an eschatological act of God may properly be affirmed in theology, and recognizes that here he stands at the opposite pole from Jaspers.[7]

As I have already suggested, Jaspers' critique of Bultmann serves to introduce the themes of his own philosophy. But before we move on to that it is worth noting the forceful and even violent resistance to all forms of religious exclusiveness which Jaspers expresses in his book *The Perennial Scope of Philosophy*. In most of his writings on the subject, Jaspers appears (both intellectually and emotionally) to stand in a love–hate relationship with revealed religion. Only in his most recent book *Philosophical Faith and Revelation* is the relationship seen in a more temperate and tender light. The ambiguous relation between philosophical faith and revealed religion is due to the factor of exclusiveness which Jaspers sees everywhere apparent in such religion, in cult, theology, personal attitudes, etc. There is a very interesting, poignant, and perhaps admonitory passage in which Jaspers expounds, at a personal level, the tenor and consequences of this exclusiveness:

Because religion is of such prime importance, awareness of my deficiency made me eager to hear what was being said in religious circles. It is among the sorrows of my life, spent in the search for truth, that discussion with theologians always dries up at crucial points; they fall silent, state an incomprehensible proposition, speak of something else, make some categoric statement, engage in amiable talk, without really taking cognizance of what one has said – and in the last analysis they are not really interested. For on the one hand they are certain of their truth, terrifyingly certain; and on the other hand they do not regard it as worth while to bother about people like us, who strike them as merely stubborn. And communication requires listening and real answers, forbids silence or the evasion of questions; it demands above all that all statements of faith (which are after all made in human language and directed towards objects, and which constitute an attempt to get one's bearings in the world) should continue to be questioned and tested, not only outwardly, but inwardly as well. No one who is in definitive possession of the truth, can speak properly with someone else – he breaks off authentic communication in favour of the belief he holds.[8]

At a more formal level, the love–hate relationship with revealed religion is found in the contrast between two propositions:

1. Biblical religion is one of the irreplaceable well-springs of philosophizing;

2. The claim to exclusivity *in* biblical religion (which is perhaps not necessary *to* biblical religion) is, in its motive and in its consequences, catastrophic for men.

Jaspers does not deny that when certain men are struck by a certain religious truth, this truth has absolute validity for them. At the same time, another truth can have absolute validity for other men. Absolute validity is therefore not universal, but historical and personal and existential. It cannot be a truth for all. On the other hand, that which is a truth for all, which has universal validity, e.g., scientific propositions, is not absolute. It is true from a certain standpoint, on the basis of a certain method, and is thus relative to both standpoint and method. If the two kinds of truth are confused, two fallacies follow:

1. the attempt to treat universally valid scientific knowledge as an absolute by which to orient one's life;

2. the attempt to treat absolute, historical faith as a universal truth for all.

It is the second of these which most concerns us here. It follows, if this second fallacy is rejected, that we cannot argue from the absolute validity of a certain truth for certain men to the universal validity of the manifestations of that truth in 'word, dogma, cult, ritual, institutions', etc.

In respect of Christianity, Jaspers regards the claim to exclusiveness as a 'fundamental perversion' bringing forth 'historical evils that wore the cloak of sacred and absolute truth'.[9] It led to religious wars, to the use of politics as a weapon of the churches, to a will to power, to a claim to world domination, and to an inquisitorial attitude towards other faiths. For all this, Jaspers insists that the claim to exclusivity does not belong to biblical religion as a whole. Indeed,

> one might venture the assertion that in the Bible seen as a whole, everything occurs in polarities. For every formulation one will ultimately find the opposite formulation. Nowhere is the whole, full, pure truth – because it cannot exist in any sentence of human speech or in any living human figure.[10]

Thus Jaspers cites polarities such as cultic religion and prophetic religion, religion of law and religion of love, the national God and the universal God. The Bible witnesses to the lived experience of such polarities, where 'passion is corrected by passion',[11] i.e., where one extreme is corrected by another extreme. Thus the Bible is the 'deposit of a thousand years of borderline experience'.

When we approach the Bible, Jaspers continues, we have to recover from these extremes, from these deviations, the truth which is always the same, even though it is never objectively and definitively present. In such a recovery we must allow that certain polarities, whatever their worth at the time, are no longer valid for, or useful to, the philosophical reflection which draws upon the Bible. Jaspers draws attention to three such fixations: national religion, the religion of the law, and the specific religion of Christ. It is the last of these that concerns us here. Of this Jaspers writes:

> we must abandon the religion of Christ, that sees God in Christ and bases the doctrine of salvation on an idea of sacrifice found in Deutero-Isaiah and applied to Christ. . . . The religion of Christ contains the truth that God speaks to man through man. But God

speaks through many men, in the Bible through the successive prophets of whom Jesus is the last. No man can be God; God speaks exclusively through no man, and what is more, his speech through every man has many meanings.[12]

Jaspers can certainly say that an implication of the biblical religion consists in the notion of 'Christ within me'. But that individual, God-given *pneuma* is not exclusively bound up with the historical Jesus. Jesus, as the God-man, is a myth. So, entirely in line with Buri's critique of Bultmann, Jaspers insists that 'the process of demythicization must not arbitrarily halt at this point'.[13]

If Jaspers is clear in his critique of exclusivism in biblical and ensuing Christian religion, he is less clear when it comes to the formulation of the shape and content of a Christian religion which does not lay claim to exclusivity. Admittedly he says:

Quite different is the Christian faith that frees itself from the exclusivist claim and its consequences.[14]

Jaspers does not pursue this matter for two reasons:

1. It is not the task of the philosopher. He can only hope to help to create the preliminary requirements for such a reformulation.

2. Jaspers insists that the transformation required must be profound.

In my first chapter I emphasized that the questions of theology have to be posed in a very special and acute way today in view of the fundamental changes in self-understanding, namely the radical shift towards the autonomy of man, which have taken place in recent centuries – changes which have accelerated in the past fifty to one hundred years. Jaspers gives full emphasis to the significance for Christian theology of this change:

What more and more people have been saying for half a century continues to be quickly forgotten, though nearly everyone has been saying it: a new era is arising, in which man, down to the very last individual, is subject to a process of transformation more radical than ever before in history. But since the transformation in our objective living conditions goes so deep, the transformations in our forms of religious belief must go correspondingly deeper in order to mould the new, to fructify and spiritualize it. A change is to be expected in what we have called the matter, the dress, the manifestation, the language of faith, a change as far-reaching as all the other changes that have taken place in our era – or else the eternal truth of biblical religion will recede beyond the horizon of man.[15]

But whatever else can or cannot be said about this transformation, it must be insisted that an integral feature will be the freeing of Christian theology from the claim to exclusivity. At this point, it is appropriate to enquire into the understanding of philosophy in general, and of ciphers in particular, which leads Jaspers to this conclusion.

I have set myself here the task of showing, briefly, how the concept of the 'cipher' as it emerges from Jaspers' total philosophical enterprise, must necessarily destroy the claim which the Christian has traditionally made for a special act of God in Christ. In a more positive way, I must also try to describe what kind of a picture emerges from Jaspers' writings when Jesus Christ is understood, not as exclusive revelation, but as one cipher among many.

There is no better way of understanding Jaspers' view of the nature of philosophy than by noting his often-repeated debt to Kierkegaard and Nietzsche, common to both of whom was their questioning of *reason*. In particular, both thinkers were gravely suspicious of the kind of truth mediated by scientific knowledge. Of course, such knowledge has a limited claim to truth, but in Kierkegaard's view, precisely this was what the learned professors did not understand. He distrusted the 'system'.

System corresponds with what is closed and settled, but existence is precisely the contrary. The philosopher of system is, as a man, like someone who builds a castle, but lives next door in a shanty.[16]

Thus for both Kierkegaard and Nietzsche, true philosophical knowledge is not the building of a system but the exercise of interpretation. This interpretation is infinite, for what has happened and has been done can always be understood in a new way: temporal life can therefore never be correctly understood by men.[17]

This view lies close to the heart of Jaspers' own conception of philosophy:

> In each individual, in all his insecurity and disquiet, philosophy must make a new start; hence it is always in process and always in suspension, it is never complete and final.[18]

We saw how Jaspers stressed that 'man is subject to a transformation more radical than ever before in history' (see above, pp. 81 f.). He also argues that Kierkegaard and Nietzsche, like no others, saw this change 'in the very substance of man'. Kierkegaard expressed his historical judgement on the very substance of his time by his *Attack upon 'Christendom'*, Nietzsche by his assertion that 'God is dead'. Jaspers' summary of the consequences can be found in the paragraph with which he begins his work *Reason and Existenz:*

> The rational is not thinkable without its other, the non-rational, and it never appears in reality without it. The only question is, in what form the other appears, how it remains in spite of all, and how it is to be grasped.[19]

Against this background we can now see the scheme of ideas in which the notion of the 'ciphers' is set. To do this, we must consider Jaspers' three-volume work *Philosophie*,[20] each volume (and indeed each chapter) of which is part of a philosophical *movement* of thought. In chronological order, the titles of the three volumes may be translated as 'Philosophical World-Orientation', 'Illumination of Existence', and 'Metaphysics'.

In the first of these, 'Philosophical World-Orientation', Jaspers is concerned to judge the scope and the limits of scientific cognition. That is to say, he deals with the knowledge of objects in space and time, with things and persons, with mathematical ideas, etc. Clearly Jaspers is not concerned with the empirical world of the sciences for its own sake. Instead, as I have said, he seeks to indicate the theoretical limits of scientific knowledge and thus to show the points at which it becomes necessary to presume a higher reality beyond. It is easy to misunderstand Jaspers at this point. He does not for a moment suggest that we can impose, in advance, limits upon scientific research into objects in this world:

> There are no restraints or limits placed upon scientific research at the intramundane level, but there are essential boundaries which it cannot trespass.[21]

At this point we observe again the powerful influence of Nietzsche upon Jaspers' whole approach to philosophy. Because he thus 'did away with knowledge', Nietzsche struck a serious blow at the notion of scientific truth as *the* unconditional truth. Science is unable to assess our passion for knowledge; this can only be done philosophically. Nor can the meaning of science be comprehended from science itself; this, too, is a philosophical problem. In other words, science cannot present us with a total world-view. It is, then, for Jaspers the task of 'Philosophical World-Orientation' to set out the limits of our scientific understanding of the world, to demarcate the points at which we must pass from 'being-as-object' to 'being-as-self' and beyond.

The second volume of Jaspers' *Philosophie* is entitled 'Illumination of Existence'. 'Existence' is a crucial word in Jaspers' philosophical vocabulary. Note that Jaspers speaks of the 'illumination' of Existence rather than of its 'description'. For unlike things in space and time, with which science deals, Existence is not an object of thought. Of course, there is a sense in which human existence is an object inasmuch, for example, as it can be studied by psychology, biochemistry, anatomy, etc. But human existence is more than this; it is also a potential for freedom of thought and action; it is the possibility of self-determination. But we can never define such things as freedom, choice and decision in the way we can define objects in the world; they can never be integrated into a system. All we can do is to point to certain categories, such as freedom, which determine Existence. It is therefore not fair just to say that Jaspers' presentation of the concept of Existence is opaque; rather, the concept defies description since it must be grasped, not conceptually, but existentially. I have stressed that, for Jaspers, Existence is always potential, is always tending towards either self-realization or failure. Above all, it is that which is potentially capable of giving itself to Transcendence. And with the introduction of the word Transcendence we enter the third phase of Jaspers' philosophical undertaking.

The third volume of his *Philosophie* is entitled 'Metaphysics'. Now it is certainly correct to say that, for Jaspers, metaphysics stands at the very centre of philosophizing. But from our reference to Nietzsche and from the brief discussion of the concept of Existence, it is clear that metaphysics must be given a very special meaning. For Jaspers, metaphysics can never be complete, final, universal, eternally valid. This is so for two reasons:

1. The questions which we ask in metaphysics are posed by a man in a concrete historical situation. Our questions are stamped by what Jaspers, and a whole tradition in German philosophy, calls 'historicity'. In other words, metaphysics has to take account of the fact of the contingent historical existence of the individual. Thus all philosophizing, as I have already said, can never lay claim to being more than the expression of the individual personality.

2. Metaphysics can never be complete or universally valid because its subject-matter, Transcendence or Being, is not an object which can be grasped conceptually.

But, says Jaspers in his 'Metaphysics', though we cannot know Transcendence, we can become aware of it. There is a link between Existence and that Transcendence which always recedes from, and escapes, our grasp.

This discussion of the relationship between personal Existence and Transcendence is one of the most difficult, yet somehow one of the most impressive and significant features of Jaspers' philosophy. It deals with what in crude and over-simplified theological terms we can translate as the relationship between man and God. It is the relationship which, in much current christian theology, is covered by the concept of revelation, whereas Jaspers' treatment of the relationship is marked again and again by a firm rejection of 'revelation' as the appropriate model. Instead, the bridge is provided by the notion of the 'cipher' or the 'cipher-script'.

If we are to understand the cipher we must bear clearly in mind that Existence cannot, according to Jaspers, *know* Transcendence (Being, God). Although we are *in relation to* Transcendence, although it is both all-encompassing and the unfathomable depth of our Existence, although Jaspers has no doubt that Transcendence 'is', nevertheless Transcendence remains unseen and unknown. It shows itself to no investigation, not even to an indirect one.[22]

On this point Jaspers is adamant. His God is without face, unrevealed. We know that he is, we do not know who he is. For we have no direct access to Transcendence whether through religious speculation or mystical union. . . . 'Thou shalt not make unto thee any image or likeness' is one of the leitmotifs of this philosophy.

Is it, then, possible to speak of God at all? Jaspers replies:

To speak of God in a philosophizing manner is not 'metaphysical speculation' but is . . . the language of a fundamental philosophical experience of faith or a basic '*existential*' act in such a fashion that God does not speak at some privileged place in space or time but rather, in so far as is possible, everywhere, yet always indirectly or ambiguously. For God is hidden, and every certainty about him is fraught with danger.[23]

At this point we begin to discern the role of ciphers. God 'speaks' (as the quotation insists) always indirectly or ambiguously, and he is 'heard' (not known) through some basic existential act. In other words, though we cannot *know* Transcendence, we can somehow be *aware* of it, we can in some sense *realize* its *presence*.

By what means, though, does Transcendence 'speak' to Existence, and Existence become 'aware' of Transcendence?

86

This is possible when we read the 'cipher-script' of Transcendence. For Jaspers, everything objective, every object, every phenomenon in the world, can be a cipher. Or, to speak more precisely, since the object is not itself the cipher, every object can have a symbolic dimension which is the cipher. Every object is a possible cipher, i.e. every object can become transparent to Transcendence. We cannot therefore say what will be a cipher. I may experience different ciphers during the course of my life. I may find that a certain cipher means one thing on one occasion and something else on another occasion. Ciphers cannot be held and kept; they are historical, instantaneous, fleeting, intermittent, fugitive. A cipher may be intelligible to one personal Existence but not to another. Two people may read the same cipher in an entirely different way. I have no criteria for judging whether a cipher is 'true'; I can only speak of it as true to the extent in which it illuminates my personal existence and brings me to personal decisions.

In the preceding paragraph I have tried, in a number of short sentences, to give an impressionistic picture of the 'cipher' and of its function. I have tried to show the essentially ambiguous and evanescent character of these ciphers as they 'speak' to my personal existence. Now this (we must understand) is the *original cipher language* as experienced uniquely and inexpressibly by my personal Existence. I look at a landscape of hill, forest and sky; I sense the beauty of colour and shape; but I also intuit something deeper even than this; I sense that this landscape is somehow more than itself; it is for my personal existence a 'cipher' of Transcendence, at that time and in that place. But – it must be repeated – the cipher is only the *language* of Transcendence. The cipher does not *symbolize* Transcendence, for that would in part mean that Transcendence was knowable. The cipher does not *embody* Transcendence, for that would make Transcendence a phenomenon, an object:

> If the reality of Transcendence is thus captured for our own reality, we have lost Transcendence . . . In actual fact we never come upon

(Transcendence). We only find its vestiges in the 'cipher-script' and this very cipher-script is the form of Being which makes Transcendence in some sense experienceable without it becoming the direct object of our cognition. The cipher-script is the *vestigium Dei*, but it is not God himself in his hiddenness. It shows us God himself as the extreme and real Being, but it does not unveil him.[24]

So far, then, we have only considered the original ciphers, experienced in a unique moment of personal existence. If this were the sum of the matter, there would be no possibility of this immediate language of the ciphers of Transcendence being communicated to, and shared by, other personal Existences. We require a more universal language of ciphers. This occurs in the symbols of, for example, myths and religion. These constitute another 'cipher-script'. But too much must not be claimed for these second-order ciphers of myths and religions. For they always depend in the last analysis upon the original cipher language immediately experienced by personal existence. No cipher can in consequence lay claim to universal truth. The ciphers are marked, as we have noted, by instability, by constant disappearance and by regeneration. And they are infinitely ambiguous, yielding different readings, each of which is in turn a cipher. They share the historicity of all Existence. If we attempt to classify them and standardize them, they fade and become 'only distantly audible'. And, further, 'with the onset of fatigue and emptiness, the ciphers lose their voice'.[25]

Now however vague the concept of cipher may be, both in Jaspers' exposition and in its own reality, there is no gainsaying the fact that ciphers are (for Jaspers) utterly crucial and central to the fact and problem of human existence:

They are that in which the whole man has a comprehensive understanding of what Being is. Therefore, cipher-reading is the primary requisite for authentic manhood.[26]

Jaspers would not suggest that our contact with the 'real' through ciphers is easy:

The one God is distant; the completely 'other' is entirely hidden. . . .

His distance makes the ascent to him almost always falter again and again. We flutter our wings of philosophizing and rise above the ground only for a few moments and only slightly.[27]

But that we can do it at all depends on the ciphers.

The concept of cipher is quite inconsistent with any final or exclusive claims for the person of Christ. This should be clear from two points which have already been made:

1. The notion of the incarnation of the deity is incompatible with Jaspers' account of Transcendence. Transcendence as incarnate, as a worldy reality, is a contradiction in terms.

2. Even if there were such a tangible revelation of God, it would be quite wrong to claim for it any exclusiveness. It would be a 'usurping by individual people and groups of people of the truth for their special historicity as having common validity for all men'.[28]

There is no cause to labour these two points; I have emphasized them repeatedly. How, then, shall we handle the myth of Jesus Christ? Jaspers' answer to the question is clear. We shall treat it as a cipher. As such, the most this myth can do is to make us aware of a hidden Transcendence. Moreover, as a cipher, it will be one among many. It can make no claim to universal validity, to absoluteness, to exclusiveness:

The one God cannot be acquired in a definite manner in an exclusive way. Only in the totality, out of historical depth, in the Encompassing of everything thinkable and everything that can be experienced, is the ascent (to God) possible.[29]

In his last major work, *Philosophical Faith and Revelation*, Jaspers somewhat modifies the extent to which revealed religion and philosophical faith are, elsewhere in his books, emphasized as polarities. He asks instead whether we may not ask the theologian to treat revelation as a cipher. What are the consequences of this for our handling of the New Testament tradition? We have to choose between the cipher

Jesus and the tangible God, Jesus Christ. If we choose the former, as Jaspers must, then the following kind of interpretation becomes appropriate:

> As a man like others, Jesus can affect everyone as cipher ... I (Jaspers) take the cipher of the cross to mean that Jesus' suffering and mortal agony ... was the result and the proof of his unprecedented, revolutionary spiritual truthfulness. ... The reality of the human Jesus is a unique, incomparable cipher of man's capacity before his God.[30] ... As a man, Jesus is a cipher of being human. It says that a man who lives and thinks as he did, a man who is true without any restriction, must die at the hands of man, because human reality is too untruthful to bear him.

This gives an indication of Jaspers' approach to Jesus as a cipher. It is clearly his view that the elaboration of his human cipher into the notion of the Son of God, and into the notion of a self-sacrificing, atoning God-man, is a perversion of the original cipher. Jaspers states bluntly:

> It takes no more than a glance at the human Jesus to disavow this evolution of the cipher. ... One thing is vital to the future of the biblical faith: to make the human Jesus and his faith prevail. Taking our bearings from Jesus makes us clearer about what we do and want. The cipher of his humanity shows us how to discover our fundamental limits and short-comings.[31]

I think there is no doubt that in this book Jaspers has conceded much to the claim of Christianity for the centrality of Jesus by his reference to Jesus as a unique, incomparable cipher of man's capacity before his God. But he has yielded nothing in his disbelief about the possibility of an incarnate God, and nothing in his disbelief about Jesus as the only mode of ascent to God. It may be that Jaspers now feels that in resisting the claim to absoluteness made for Jesus, he has previously gone to the other extreme of minimizing the importance of Jesus as a cipher. Elsewhere Jaspers has written:

> Philosophy must guard against usurpation while recognizing at the same time a cipher truth in the claims of the usurper.[32]

He appears especially to have heeded the second part of this prescription in his most recent handling of Christian revelation:

> The contents of claimed revelation, when stripped of their absolutisms and their character of exclusiveness, are to be adopted philosophically in the form of ciphers.[33]

However, if Jaspers is true to his own account of ciphers, there is no reason to assume that he would regard his own reading of the cipher of Jesus as complete or definitive. Moreover, he would say, as always, that he philosophizes from his personal viewpoint, which is that of one reared in a Christian (Protestant) tradition. The cipher of Jesus will seem quite different for those who belong to another tradition. For, has Jaspers not insisted, ciphers are endlessly ambiguous and can be read in endless ways. But the manner in which, according to Jaspers, this incomparable cipher is to be read is surely clear. It must be read on the premise that 'Jesus is, to be sure, not God in the world. No man is God'.[34]

There is insufficient space to criticize Jaspers at length here. It is, however, possible to relate some of his viewpoints to those that we have already considered. In particular, there are some formal similarities between the standpoints of Jaspers and Ogden, particularly in relation to Bultmann.

1. For Ogden, Christian faith is to be interpreted solely in existential terms as man's original possibility of authentic self-understanding independent of any particular historical occurrence. In a similar way, Jaspers could make the same claim for philosophical faith.

2. Ogden insists that Christian faith is always a possibility in fact because of the unconditional gift and demand of God's love, which is the ever-present ground and end of all created things. Jaspers would say in turn that it is only possible to speak of Existence at all because of Transcendence. Transcendence is, moreover, always open for the movement of Existence towards it.

But the gulf between Ogden and Jaspers arises concerning the claim which Ogden makes for Jesus Christ in relation to the possibility of authentic existence. Whereas Ogden can say that Jesus is the decisive manifestation of the divine love, fulfilling and correcting all others, Jaspers would not find it possible to say that the cipher of the human Jesus is the decisive pointer to Transcendence, nor, consequently, could he say that it fulfils and corrects all other ciphers. We have seen that Jaspers does concede the Jesus-cipher to be unique and incomparable, though we must be cautious about the weight that we give to these words. Compared with the comprehensive claims made for Jesus Christ by Christian theology, Jaspers' claim for Jesus is limited to a very particular area. Again, Ogden writes that men can realize their true life as men *only* if they understand themselves in the way concretely represented to them in Jesus' word and deed and tragic destiny. For Jaspers, this 'only' must be a stumbling block. No one cipher can lead to God. Only in the totality, out of historical depth, is the ascent possible. The reading of ciphers is, for the individual, a regular activity at all levels of his life.

> Thus the grasp of Being through the ciphers is never achieved and once for all, but is a constant movement, an incessant conquest and recurrent loss.[35]

To say in any way 'only in Jesus' must involve an illegitimate fixation, standardization, absolutizing, and even degradation of the cipher involved. Ogden, for all his own penetrating criticism and development of Bultmann's position, still remains more in the camp of Bultmann than in that of Jaspers.

In the next chapter I shall examine the work of a theologian who believes that nevertheless Jaspers' scheme can be put to fruitful use in posing the question about Jesus Christ.

NOTES

1. H.-W. Bartsch (ed.), *Kerygma and Myth* II, London 1962, p. 179.

2. *Op. cit.*, p. 135.
3. *Op. cit.*, p. 137.
4. *Op. cit.*, p. 166.
5. *Op. cit.*, p. 171.
6. *Op. cit.*, p. 146.
7. *Op. cit.*, p. 193.
8. Karl Jaspers, *The Perennial Scope of Philosophy*, London 1950, pp. 77 f.
9. *Op. cit.*, p. 92.
10. *Op. cit.*, p. 97.
11. *Op. cit.*, p. 101.
12. *Op. cit.*, p. 103.
13. *Op. cit.*, p. 104.
14. *Op. cit.*, p. 94.
15. *Op. cit.*, pp. 106 f.
16. Jaspers, *Reason and Existenz*, London 1956, p. 26.
17. *Op. cit.*, p. 27.
18. Paul A. Schilpp (ed.), *The Philosophy of Karl Jaspers*, New York 1957, p. 96.
19. *Reason and Existenz*, p. 19.
20. 3 vols., Berlin 1932.
21. *The Philosophy of Karl Jaspers*, p. 126.
22. Xavier Tilliette, *Karl Jaspers*, Paris 1960, pp. 54 f.
23. *The Philosophy of Karl Jaspers*, p. 784.
24. *Op. cit.*, p. 673.
25. Jaspers, *Philosophical Faith and Revelation*, London 1967, p. 107.
26. Jaspers, *Truth and Symbol*, London 1959, p. 50.
27. *Op. cit.*, p. 72.
28. *Op. cit.*, p. 76.
29. *Op. cit.*, p. 78.
30. *Philosophical Faith and Revelation*, p. 338.
31. *Ibid.*
32. *Truth and Symbol*, p. 77.
33. *Op. cit.*, p. 76.
34. *Ibid.*
35. *The Philosophy of Karl Jaspers*, p. 108.

6 Relating the Symbol of Christ to our Existence

In an earlier chapter I mentioned some of the objections raised by the Basel theologian Fritz Buri against Bultmann's retention of a unique and exclusive divine act of salvation in Christ. These objections do not, however, give us an adequate account of Buri's later approach to the question of Jesus Christ. First, they are essentially a negative response to another position and contain only brief indications of Buri's own independent approach. Secondly, since they were made, in 1952, Buri has expanded and developed his own thinking in a way which in many respects goes far beyond his earlier works.

Around the mid-fifties there appeared in his writings an important shift of emphasis. Until this time his thinking had been dominated by Albert Schweitzer's approach to Jesus as outlined in the final pages of *The Quest of the Historical Jesus*. He shared the related view of Martin Werner that the whole of early Christian theology was affected by the failure of the Second Coming to take place.[1]

On this basis, Buri made two points:

1. Schweitzer's approach of 'consistent eschatology' not only revealed the perils of modernizing Jesus, as this had been carried out by nineteenth-century liberal theologians, but also dealt a death-blow to the dogmatic theory of the 'two natures' of Jesus Christ:

The only distinctive feature about Jesus in relation to this
common expectation was the passion with which he looked
forward to the Parousia. But in this expectation he was, as
history showed, mistaken.

2. Granted that the theory of 'two natures' was a mistake,
and granted that the eschatological Christ was a common
myth in the culture to which Jesus belonged, the myth
nevertheless had certain important features, which, once
recognized to be symbolical rather than objective in
character, constructively assist the attempt to arrive at an
existential account of Christology. As we have already seen
from Buri's dispute with Bultmann, the eschatological myth
could *not* be used to support any theory of a unique and
objective divine act occurring in Jesus' death and resurrection. Such a theory would have to depend on the assertion
that somehow or other the 'end' *did* begin with Jesus' death
and resurrection. But the non-appearance of the Parousia
showed that there was no end to begin! Bultmann's attempt
to demythologize the cross and resurrection from being a
cosmic eschatological event to become an *existential*
eschatological event is therefore a wholly mistaken venture.
There is in the New Testament nothing validly eschatological
for Bultmann to demythologize. This leads to the more
general conclusion:

> The salvation-event does not consist in a once-for-all saving work of
> Christ ... The salvation-event is not limited to the New Testament
> or the Bible or the Christian community. Salvation does not depend
> on *one* point in history. To the degree that the New Testament says
> so, it is mythological talk no longer relevant to us.[3]

In the mid-fifties, Buri's position changed. I will not
attempt to document this change in detail except to note
that Schweitzer's consistent eschatology recedes, Werner

comes under criticism and the star of Jaspers is in the ascendant. The effect of this 'turn' in Buri's thought may be seen, for example, in the first volume of his *Dogmatik*.[4] In that volume Buri still reserves serious criticism for the Chalcedonian Christology, but he does not appeal to Schweitzer in so doing. Buri continues, and greatly develops, his project of an existential interpretation of Christology, but it is no longer an eschatological Christ-myth which is interpreted. Instead, under the influence of form-critical approaches, Buri stresses the kerygmatic nature of the New Testament documents as themselves engaged in and requiring existential interpretation. There is, I think, little doubt that the main explanation for this shift of thought lies with Buri's rapidly increasing preoccupation with Karl Jaspers' philosophy. For with the different Christological discussion, in the second volume of the *Dogmatik*, we must link the epistemological discussion which comes in the first volume and in many of Buri's later writings. The upshot of this epistemological discussion is, as we shall see, to determine in advance that the New Testament kerygma must be handled according to the pattern of Jasper's philosophizing.

In the course of this new orientation Buri's theology has gained immensely in stature. The way that he grounds his existential account of Christian belief is no longer based upon the acceptance of a particular theory (i.e. Schweitzer's consistent eschatology) – a theory which leads Buri into some very suspect New Testament exegesis, and which is hardly ever likely to prove acceptable to New Testament scholars in the form set out by Schweitzer and used by Werner. Instead, Buri's theology must stand or fall on acceptance or rejection of his general epistemological foundations, to which he has given more and more attention in recent years.

In addition, it should be said that a full picture of Buri's handling of Christology must await the publication of the third volume of his *Dogmatik*. None the less, the direction of his thought in this respect is clear, and its consequences for understanding the question of Jesus Christ are equally clear.

Buri's little catechism *Unterricht im christlichen Glauben* (*Instruction in the Christian Faith*)[5] serves as a useful pointer to the shape of his theology. It is divided into five main sections, of which the subject-matter and the order of presentation is significant:

1. Knowledge, Faith and Revelation;
2. Man and sin;
3. Reconciliation through Christ;
4. God and his Creation;
5. The Church and the Kingdom of God.

The main purpose of the first section is to clarify the meaning of knowledge and faith, and this is done in an empirical fashion without explicit appeal to either theism or Christology. In a way which reminds us of the first volume of Jaspers' *Philosophie*, Buri seeks, as quickly as possible, to get to the point where we can distinguish between that which can be known objectively and that which has to be grasped non-objectively. This is the nub of his distinction between knowledge and faith. It is apparent, therefore, that 'faith' is not in the first place a specifically theological concept but a general human attitude to one aspect of the reality in which we are set. We can note Buri's movement of thought in this respect by quoting the titles of the first four articles in this section of the catechism:

How are knowledge, faith and revelation related in the Christian tradition?

What difficulties result from these traditional concepts of the relation between knowledge, faith and revelation?

What, and how, can we in fact know?

Are there impassable limits to our knowledge?

These theses can be developed from the epistemological sections in Buri's other writings. The first point that Buri wishes to make is that the very act of thought involves us in a subject–object relationship:

> When I begin to think, I think something; and as long as I think, I do not escape this I–object relationship.[6]

I am a subject to this world of objects. From the outset Buri wants to emphasize that in talking both about knowledge *and* faith, we are dealing with something 'objective' – to use this word loosely for the moment. At the very beginning Buri thus seeks to answer the common charge that an existentialist philosophy falls prey to 'mere subjectivism':

> But even though I and the object are inextricably connected to each other, we never exchange places with the object of our thinking, not even when we think about ourselves.[7]

What, then, are the respective 'objects' of knowledge and faith?

In respect of knowledge, the answer is simple. The subject-matter of the exact sciences furnishes the objects for knowledge. But there are two limits (and again we are reminded of Jaspers' 'World-Orientation') beyond which cognition cannot go, two absolute and unconditional limits. These limits are the self and the totality of Being:

> 1. The subject, the thinking 'I' can never be made the object of thinking;
> 2. The totality of Being, the totality of the spiritual world, the totality of reality, the entirety of nature, is unattainable as an object.[8]

We do not therefore 'know' the self and Being; they are not objects of cognition in the normal sense.[9] At the same time they are, as it were, 'real'; they are not just inventions; we do think about them.[10] So the problem arises: if, as thinking beings, we can never escape the subject–object scheme, how can we think and talk about the 'self' and 'Being', which are not objects? Buri's answer to this question serves as one of the main clues to his theological and Christological method. It is indeed impossible, in his view, to escape the subject–object pattern. But, for this very reason, Buri is very critical of those who would attempt to solve the problem of thinking about the non-objectifiable by seeking out a non-objectifying form of thinking. For 'thinking always thinks about something'.[11]

Buri's answer to this problem revolves around the notion of 'symbol'. A symbol is the way in which something non-objective can be present to us. The symbol *points* to the non-objective. So, if we cannot think about the non-objective as such, we can think about the symbol which points to the non-objective. This faith (the thinking which transcends) can turn to the symbol as the objectivity of the non-objective.

We shall return later to Buri's use of this argument in respect of Christology. For the present, however, we must further explore how Buri characterizes these two areas – the self and Being – which in themselves fall beyond the limits of knowledge, in the realm of faith.

1 *The Self*

Obviously we have been stamped and defined in our entire being through our past and by our environment. Yet, *we* are still what we are, and it is *we* who continually determine what we are through the way we understand ourselves.[12] For Buri, therefore, selfhood or personhood is constituted above all by 'responsibility' – a key-word in his theological vocabulary. 'I' am 'responsible personhood' inasmuch as I determine what I am through the way in which I understand myself. But this responsible personhood eludes being made into an object of thought. Responsible personhood is not something I can point to; it is rather something which 'occurs' as I enact responsibility, as I take responsibility upon myself. This personhood cannot be an object in the normal sense. It is not a part of me; it is something total which encompasses and permeates my entire existence. Thus, strictly speaking, we cannot describe the 'nature' of man as if it were an object. By accepting our destiny of being, that being which in each case has to decide what he will be, we *experience* the nature of man.[13] This, then, is the first limit to objectification – the self.

99

Not just in our innermost 'I', but likewise at the widest horizons of our physical and spiritual cosmos, we come up against that mystery which announces itself at the limits of our objective knowledge. . . . Here in the midst of the richness of the cognitive world of objectivity, a nothingness is revealed, revealed not to that desire for knowledge which stops short and settles for provisional results, but to that which always asks more and seeks further and further. Absolutely no statement can be made concerning this nothingness because it retreats before every attempt to grasp it objectively.[14]

If we regard Being as an object it is, therefore, nothingness; if we think of ourselves as finite objects on the way to death we encounter nothingness. But, if we decide on responsible selfhood, if we decide that we shall be responsible for determining what we shall be, we can then take a leap beyond objectivity and we can become aware that nothingness is not the only face of Being. This notion of a leap, a jumping-off point, derives from what Jaspers calls the 'turnabout' (*Umwendung*):

When we sense that the world is bottomless, that our origin is unfathomable, that humanity, this eye and light in the dark universe, this voice in an otherwise silent world, is unique – when we doubt ourselves in our freedom that is not self-made but a gift from elsewhere – then the basic philosophical operation gives us room, so to speak, to find a place and a point for everything.[15]

In this quotation, Jaspers characterizes the 'turnabout' not least as a sense that our freedom is not self-made, but is a *gift* from elsewhere. This is an extremely important qualification to Jaspers' frequent emphasis upon the autonomy of man. Jaspers makes the same point, in an impressive way, in *Philosophical Faith and Revelation*. If freedom is the basic experience of responsible self-being, then with the realization of this freedom we realize that it is not self-made but granted. The more decisive our certainty of our freedom, the greater our certainty of the Transcendence we owe it to.[16] In a sentence, 'It is not through myself that I am'.[17] Buri picks up this notion of Existence as 'gift' and employs it for his own theological purposes in two ways.

First, it is a stick with which to beat, for example, Bultmann. Existence as such, not one exclusive divine act, is grace. This point I have already mentioned. But at least as important is the fact that this notion enables Buri to endorse the traditional Christian claim that 'salvation' is 'from above', not of man.

Admittedly we can never minimize the fact that we are surrounded by nothingness. Everything perishes, and man's history is filled with tribulation. But as we take the leap of responsible personhood, we can become aware of Being as a gift, as an opportunity given to us which is to be grasped and actualized at every moment. To describe this 'Being as a gift', Buri also employs the term 'grace':

> Man who experiences himself abandoned into Nothingness perceives even in his impotence a power which summons him to responsibility. This is a power which places man's existence at his own disposal, as that realm of Being assigned to him for the actualization of responsible life.

Then Buri goes on to give a new turn to the concept of 'faith':

> We designate as *faith* the act of becoming aware of this situation in which we become conscious of our responsibility and of the mystery of Being and through which consciousness we come to ourselves. . . . For such faith, Being is grace in that it gives to man the possibility of actualizing this responsibility which constitutes his essence.[18]

Buri, then, uses the idea of Being as a gift, as grace, to safeguard the theological truth that man is not his own redeemer, the truth that we do not simply *see* the world as the sphere of our responsible existence, but that the world is *disclosed* to us as the sphere of our responsible existence. Buri expresses this 'otherness' in different ways. He calls it, poetically, a voice:

> Out of this nothingness, personhood becomes aware of the voice which calls it to responsibility and discloses to it space and time, a whole world of objectivity, as the place and the opportunity for the realization of responsibility.[19]

Or he can characterize the gift-nature of this summons as a 'surprise':

101

It comes to us as a surprise, just as God in the mythical stories surprised men with his summons with which they must struggle and through the obedience or disobedience to which either salvation or judgement occurred.

We can interpret cosmological and other myths to gain the same insight. Thus the Genesis narrative insists that man is creator neither of himself nor of his world. He does not speak the creative word. He can only hear the voice and take over the dominion he has been given.[20] The doctrine of creation thus means:

the understanding of space and time as the opportunity for the actualization of that personhood to which we are summoned.[21]

At the same time, Buri will not countenance any doctrine of fallenness or original sin which might suggest that we are incapable of responding to this summons, this voice. This would be to deny his own central category of responsibility. Man, still an unfinished creature, can attain and actualize himself. Sin is the act by which we pervert our responsible personhood into its contrary,[22] not a flaw which denies to man the possibility of choosing to implement his own destiny.

Thus, the summons to responsible personhood is given with Being, though never as an object. So we depend upon religious cosmologies, myths, etc., for the hearing of this summons. For these contain symbols which, as we have seen, point to the non-objective. As Buri writes in his Catechism:

We can only speak of the mysteries of revelation in pictures, which, as the language of faith, point to the inexpressible, but which can be understood in their truth only by him who has faith.[23]

Buri is here entirely in accord with the structure of Jaspers' thinking about ciphers. We read the language of Being in cipher-script (Jaspers); we discern the summons of God only in symbols (Buri).

It is at this point that we begin to see Buri's attitude to the question about Jesus Christ. The problem arises in this

102

way. Buri has insisted that the summons to responsibility belongs to Being as grace:

So long as there are men, there will also be responsibility, and with it the voice which summons to responsibility: 'Adam, where art thou?'.[24]

On the other hand, in Christian theology this voice is identified with the word of God made flesh, namely Jesus Christ. What is the relation between this universal summons and the particularity and historicality of Jesus Christ?

Buri gives in his many writings for the most part a consistent answer to this question, though his means of arriving at it varies. For him the New Testament message of Christ the redeemer is completely bound up with the hearing of this voice which summons us to realize our destiny as responsible persons. But we must bear in mind that it is God, and God alone, who is the power who summons us to responsibility and gives us the possibility for its actualization. The mythology of the Christ must therefore be regarded as a symbol of this summons and this possibility. The task of theology, then, is not to invent a new picture of Christ, but rather to understand the pictures of Christ in the tradition as symbols of existence as grace.

Where the influence of Schweitzer and Werner have receded, Buri turns less to the eschatological myth of the Christ than to the character of the New Testament writings in order to justify his interpretation. He summarizes his mature intention in this way:

The problem involved in Christology can only be overcome and rendered fruitful when Christology is seen as an expression of the self-understanding of Christian faith, and thus as an expression of personal truth.[25]

The speculative constructions of the Fathers, the attempts (e.g. in Schleiermacher and Ritschl) to view Jesus as a religious personality – these and other theories founder through the knowledge, which now comes to us from New

103

Testament scholarship, of the kerygmatic character of the New Testament writings. The New Testament is a witness of faith and, as such, it cannot be employed as an historical source. This insight meets the complementary philosophical insight into the historicity of all statements about man which also shows these statements to be objectively indemonstrable. So we can say that, in the primitive Christian kerygma concerning the divine act of salvation, there is expressed a particular relation to Transcendence on the part of Christian faith. (This is a reference to Jaspers' notion of 'relatedness to Transcendence'.) When the Christian affirms that through Christ he understands himself as a new creature, then for him God-in-Christ is in a certain way revealed and active, in a manner which he had known and experienced nowhere else. But this relation to Transcendence, it must be stressed, happens neither in a supernatural revealed dogma, nor on the plane of natural reason, nor in an experience which can be grasped psychologically; it happens in *human personhood*, as Buri has described it.

Now it must have become perfectly clear from this discussion that Buri cannot allow that this summons to responsible personhood is exclusively bound up with Jesus Christ. This is evident, Buri holds, from the New Testament itself.

Even the New Testament record does not restrict the locus of the Christ merely to Jesus but suggests a much wider dominion.[26]

However impressive the Christ-myth may be as a symbol of such an understanding of existence, it is only *a* symbol.

Buri deals at length with the question of symbols. Closely reflecting Jaspers' treatment of ciphers, Buri insists on the absolute necessity of symbols as means of presenting to us those realities which cannot in themselves be objectified. When, therefore, I say 'only a symbol' I have no intention of minimizing their importance. Instead, I wish to emphasize that no symbol can be regarded as absolute. Thus the event of self-understanding is not bound up with either Jesus or the mythology of the Christ:

> However powerful historically the Christian ideas and concepts have become for this redeeming self-understanding, its content is not bound to these historical forms.

On the contrary

> *this event occurs wherever man understands himself as absolutely responsible and experiences the fulfilment of his destiny* [my italics] ... Certainly this viewpoint is not limited to Jesus Christ and the realm of symbols and sensibility connected to his name.

It is quite legitimate for us as Christians to describe this becoming-aware of absolute responsibility as 'being-in-Christ', as long as this being-in-Christ is not necessarily bound to the appearance of Jesus nor to the historical results which have emanated from him.[27] There will always be the serious danger that the Christian tradition will require us to be obedient to its own historically conditioned myth rather than to that voice (of God) to which alone we are responsible. This will be to commit the error (noted, as we saw, by Jaspers) of treating the historically contingent as universally true.

Buri believes that the New Testament does not make this mistake. For the New Testament, the Christ is not bound to any one historical form but is the Logos of God. We may use the expression 'the Christ' as a cipher for that voice which calls us to responsibility, but we can never declare as indispensable, as necessary to salvation, one specific appearance in history; we can never assert that its historicity should be binding on all.

In this respect, the second volume of Buri's *Dogmatik* makes very interesting reading. At first sight it seems as if his concentration upon the traditional Christian symbols (the image of God, the deity and the humanity of Christ, etc.) contradicts the point which we have just made. This is not, however, the case. On the contrary, Buri's actual interpretation of these symbols follows his appointed method. God's becoming man in Christ corresponds to man's becoming man as the perception of personal being before the personal God. Similarly, the manhood of the 'God-man' emphasizes symbolically the reality of personhood, in the same way as the deity of the 'God-man' is a cipher of relatedness to Transcendence. Here Buri appears more appreciative than before of the remarkable intensity of the major Christian symbols. As we saw, a similar appreciation developed in Jaspers. Perhaps once he has established the principle that no appeal to the exclusive character of Christian revelation may be allowed, he no longer has a bad conscience about exploring deeply and positively those symbols which are, from a historical viewpoint, specifically Christian.

Certainly Buri would insist that Christianity is not required to deny its myth, nor indeed (as Christian history makes clear) can it do without it. What is more, the proclamation of the message of Christ can be the occasion for men becoming aware of their unconditional responsibility. All this is perfectly acceptable as long as we avoid the danger of making the one cipher absolute for all. Nothing must count against the fact that it is God who is the power who summons us to responsibility and gives us the possibility for its actualization, and that this possibility is open to all.

I have emphasized that, according to Buri, none of these qualifications make it necessary for us to minimize the effect of the Christ kerygma for us. In one place, Buri says that the Christ-cipher is, in intensity, 'hardly surpassable' as an expression of existence as grace. Again, in his *Catechism*, he remarks:

The Cross of Christ becomes for us the decisive salvation-event, whenever we understand ourselves, in him, as co-crucified and as appointed to new life.[28]

There is no need to minimize this and pretend that what is decisive for us is not decisive for us. But we are not licensed to say that it must be the same for all:

The Christian may say 'only in Christ', so long as this represents not an exclusive claim understood to have universal validity but a meaningful affirmation of the redemptive possibility available in the Christian message.... Awareness of the meaning of life as 'the reception of oneself as a gift' does not belong exclusively to any one tradition, though Christians may, because of their heritage, actualize it themselves within the Judeo-Christian context.[29]

One major comment in conclusion. Van Harvey writes:

I do not mean that men are made whole (that is, righteous) by believing certain propositions about Jesus or God or by engaging in certain disciplines. I mean, rather, that men are made free only when they attain the basic confidence that the reality which sustains them can be trusted, that life is a gift, that there is a giver, and that men are called upon to assume responsibility for the world that has been given to them.... But though I came to believe that Christian affirmations are, to use the current jargon, 'existential', I have not been able to reject out of hand all attempts to delineate 'objectively' the content of these affirmations.... I do not yet see why these realities which impinge upon us 'existentially' cannot also be reflected upon dispassionately and philosophically; why under certain conditions and reasons a 'Thou' may not be thought about as an 'it'.... For these and other reasons, I have always been more sympathetic to theologies which are empirical, in the sense of continually trying to relate Christian symbols to the structures of men's actual existence.[30]

This is a good account of the positive contribution of Buri's theology. But is Buri's scheme sufficiently comprehensive in character to reflect adequately the scope of that threefold evidence to which I have more than once referred? As in the case of Bultmann and, to a lesser degree, Ogden, Buri's treatment of Jesus Christ is severely restricted to the framework of personal being. What is the reason for this, and what consequences are entailed by it?

Buri (along with Bultmann) holds what can only be called an 'iron-curtain' theory of knowledge. In Buri's case, this is based on Jaspers' rigid distinction between being an object and being a self. In fact there is nothing particularly original about this distinction, which is part of the stock-in-trade of many theologians and philosophers in this century, though no one has expounded it as clearly or as carefully as Jaspers.

Bultmann again and again insists on the irrelevance for faith of speculative reasoning and of the human and natural sciences: for example, eschatology must have nothing to do with the final destination of the world. Buri counters any suggestion that more objectivity should be given to Bultmann's scheme by insisting that such a move would confuse the distinction between 'world' and 'Existence'.

Now this emphasis on personal existence as *the* context for Christian theology is, as I have already argued, to be taken very seriously. Theology is surely concerned above all with personhood, and whatever our view of revelation, it consists in *our* words, *our* images, *our* faltering speech about the actualization of our lives as human beings before God. But it is surely possible to emphasize personal existence as *the* context for theology without putting it in a watertight compartment within which 'knowledge' is gained in one way, and outside which 'knowledge' is gained in an entirely different way.

Earlier (see p. 66), we met the suggestion that a simple view of existential knowledge is not acceptable, and that we must distinguish between 'subjective' and 'objective' modes within that knowledge. At the same time we have to reckon with the fact that scientific understanding has undergone many transformations in recent decades and that scientific positivism is now widely discredited. Thus in scientific knowledge, too, we have surely to discern both 'subjective' and 'objective' modes in close relation; to realize (for example) that the old picture of scientific method as 'verification and proof, but not discovery', is a travesty.

I quoted Van Harvey to the effect that we should continually try to relate Christian symbols to the structures of man's actual existence. Buri would indeed share such a concern. But on an iron-curtain view of knowledge, only a limited dimension of the 'structures of man's actual existence' can be discovered. Surely within these structures we must include man's relationship, as an evolutionary species, to the natural order; man's discovery of his past, through the exercise of the historian's craft, and through archaeology, paleontology and the like; and man's perception of his present social existence through social psychology, sociology, etc. It was Troeltsch's view that modern historical science had above all revealed to us the richness and profusion of historical life. In contrast, it is hard to escape the impression that Jaspers and Buri present us with a very formal and generalized view of Existence. Both Jaspers' ciphers and Buri's symbols seem to lack embodiment and richness of texture. They seem victims of excessive abstraction and generalization. Buri has been criticized for the *formal* quality of his theological categories. This is not, however, a personal quirk on Buri's part, nor simply a matter of theological style. It stems ultimately, in my opinion, from the iron-curtain theory of knowledge which I have described. In contrast, the recognition that there are windows between 'being a self' and 'being an object' can surely lead to symbols being given a much more concrete and substantive content. I recognize that this may appear to open the flood-gates to those who would emphasize that man is 'nothing but' an advanced ape and who would deny his personhood. But this risk must be taken. I do not believe that Buri's 'symbol' will fulfil its potential unless he recognizes that the symbol cannot be confined to the categories of Existence – rich and profound as these are – but must also draw more seriously upon the total environment in which Existence is set and of which it is a part.

For the formality and abstraction of Buri's symbols, and his system's lack of contact with that reality which lies beyond the sphere of personhood, is not only based (as I believe) upon a misjudgement about the intentions and possibilities of contemporary scientific enquiry (using 'scientific' in its widest sense); it also goes against the seriousness with which many people do in fact regard the world as a subject of theological concern. When, for example, Buri interprets creation as 'the understanding of space and time as the opportunity for the actualization of that personhood to which we are summoned', he is surely guilty of the one-sidedness to which I have referred. To interpret the manifold richness of the material order which we are coming to know, and in some respect beginning to control, as simply the spatio-temporal opportunity for the realization of personhood, seems to me an astonishing example of reductionism. It is clear that people *do* ask as to the meaning of that spatio-temporal world and are not satisfied to say that the detailed inductive knowledge of that world must in principle be irrelevant to an enquiry about personal-being.

Men are concerned to reflect upon the origin and the destiny of their species, and of the cosmos in which their world is set. They are concerned to ask about the future prospects of *homo sapiens* beyond the stage of evolutionary development which he has now reached. How are, for, example, eschatological symbols to be related to such enquiries? Are they to be interpreted solely in terms of man's call to responsible personhood in the present? Or do they not have some temporal and futurist dimension as symbols calling man to the personalizing and responsible development of the space–time continuum in which he is set? And cannot such symbols therefore also be interpreted as symbols of the hope which Being sets before man in his passage through the world in a process of time? Must not Existence as grace have something in view?

It seems to me one of the most serious consequences of the iron-curtain theory of knowledge that personal being is not set, by Jaspers or Buri, within a moving sequence of psychological, social, natural and cosmic history, but rather in the context of punctilinear personal history. I fully realize that there are dangers in the proposals which I am making for the enrichment of Buri's theological enterprise, but I am firmly convinced that the judicious interrelating of different modes, levels and fruits of our knowledge is essential if Christian proclamation is really to move men of a so-called secular age to the shouldering of that responsible personhood which Buri so rightly and so remarkably evokes.

So we have to ask again whether these wider perspectives must not be kept in view when we ask the question about Jesus Christ.

NOTES

1. Martin Werner, *The Formation of Christian Dogma*, London 1957.

2. F. Buri, *Christian Faith in Our Time*, New York 1966, p. 82. (The German version was published in 1952.)

3. H.-W. Bartsch (ed.), *Kerygma und Mythos* II, p. 97.

4. F. Buri, *Dogmatik als Selbstverständnis des christlichen Glaubens*, Vol. 2, Bern 1962.

5. Bern 1957.

6. F. Buri, *Thinking Faith*, Philadelphia 1968, p. 5.

7. *Op. cit.*, p. 6.

8. *Op. cit.*, pp. 12 f.

9. *Op. cit.*, p. 13.

10. *Op. cit.*, p. 58.

11. In E. Käsemann *et al.*, *Distinctive Protestant and Catholic Themes Reconsidered*, New York 1967, p. 144.

12. In *Andover Newton Theological Quarterly*, Vol. 8, p. 130. See also F. Buri, *How can we still speak responsibly of God?*, Philadelphia 1968.

13. *Thinking Faith*, p. 28.

14. *Andover Newton Quarterly*, p. 132.

15. Karl Jaspers, *Philosophical Faith and Revelation*, pp. 77 f.

16. *Op. cit.*, p. 95.

17. Jaspers, *The Perennial Scope of Philosophy*, p. 67.

18. Buri, *Thinking Faith*, p. 46.

19. *Andover Newton Quarterly* p. 133.

20. *Ibid.*

21. *Thinking Faith*, p. 100.

22. *Ibid.*

23. *Unterricht*, p. 22.

24. *Andover Newton Quarterly*, p. 133.

25. In *Neue Zeitschrift für systematische Theologie* I, 1959, p. 153.

26. *Christian Faith in Our Time*, p. 95.

27. *Andover Newton Quarterly*, p. 135.

28. *Unterricht*, p. 55.

29. H. H. Oliver, *The Journal of Bible and Religion* XXXIV, 1966, pp. 355, 357.

30. In Dean Peerman (ed.), *Frontline Theology*, pp. 109 ff.

7   Christ in the World of Matter

The power of the Word Incarnate penetrates matter itself; it goes down into the deepest depths of the lower forces.[1]

These words from *Le Milieu Divin* by Pierre Teilhard de Chardin add to the question about Jesus Christ a dimension largely absent from the work of the authors so far discussed. To a greater or lesser extent, those authors shied away from questions not derived from the structure of our personal existence. It is true that process philosophy does to some considerable extent expound this wider dimension, though we observed that this was hardly brought out in Ogden's use of that resource for his talk about Jesus Christ. Ernst Troeltsch also moved out boldly into the relativities of world-history, but defined it as (for the most part) cultural history. While recognizing that this history is profoundly conditioned by natural phenomena, Troeltsch betrays in his thinking little or no contact with the world of the natural sciences. This may best be explained on the grounds that he saw the natural sciences as closely bound up with a positivistic world-view and as committed to a generalizing method which suppresses that individual trait which is the basic feature of history. All the same, Troeltsch's brief but serious ventures into speculative thought, exploring the theme of the One and the Many, show that he was searching for a way of affirming that the reality in which we are set is not to be be understood exhaustively in terms of the determinism and strict causality of the sciences of his day, but in terms of process, movement and interrelatedness. Thus his own historical categories of individuality and development are somehow writ large across the entire face of reality.

At the end of the previous chapter, I indicated the violence done to common sense if we effect a radical breach between questions about personal existence on the one hand, and scientific questions on the other. It is, however, understandable that, where secular thought has fostered a strongly positivistic approach to science, theology should over-react, in the interests of survival, by itself claiming a great gulf between the subject-matter of theology and the subject-matter of the sciences. Equally, it is hardly surprising that the account of Jesus Christ, given on this basis, should be narrowly confined to personal categories and should be presented as making a greater appeal to faith by virtue of its very indemonstrability. However, as part of the evidence against which we ask the question about Jesus Christ, we now have to reckon with what has been called 'an effort towards synopticism' among no small number of scientists and philosophers of science.[2]

In this chapter I want to examine briefly the way in which questions can be asked about Jesus Christ when some such framework as this is employed. To illustrate my discussion I have selected certain themes from the work of Pierre Teilhard de Chardin (1881–1955) which I regard as a particularly interesting example of this approach. At the outset we must observe that Teilhard's enterprise is informed by a careful balance between two starting-points – a balance which he regards as mandatory for anyone who regards himself as a Christian and as a man of the modern age – namely the scientific understanding of our evolutionary world and the witness of the Christian tradition (including the Bible) to Jesus Christ. It was Teilhard's profoundly held conviction that these two resources can never be separated if we are to attain to an adequate vision of the reality in which we are set. At this point Teilhard's thought is at its most seminal and its most vulnerable, since he holds that we must be able to pass from one mode of knowledge to another, from the data of reason to the data of Christian belief, with confidence and without confusion.

The model constructed by Teilhard for this purpose is

not that of a general, static and comprehensive idea within which we can contain all particular ideas. He develops instead a *dialectic* which can come to terms not only with the overall harmony of the universe but also with the real and many tensions which are indubitably part of that overall picture. Teilhard's account of Jesus Christ must, at every point, be seen in the light of this dialectic. Thus (for example) on the one hand Teilhard can, with his Christian belief, postulate an end-in-Christ for all created things; on the other hand he can, with his generalizations from scientific data, postulate a convergent evolution. Only on the basis of his dialectic, however, can he relate the one to the other. Again, on the one hand scientific knowledge exposes the restricted context of the Church's teaching about Jesus Christ. On the other hand, Christian belief itself furnishes a wider perspective against which that scientific knowledge must be seen. Thus Teilhard sets himself the task of working out a *dynamic* relationship between Christian faith and cosmic evolution. If, therefore, Christian faith affirms that Jesus Christ in God is the author and end of all things, such a notion must now be inserted within the dimensions of cosmic evolution. For this purpose, Teilhard explores the notion of a *co-extensiveness* between the dimensions of Christ and the dimensions of the universe. It was thus that Teilhard withstood what he regarded as the great temptation of the century (and of the hour), namely that of 'finding the world of nature, life and humanity greater, nearer, more mysterious and more living than the God of Scripture'.[3] Teilhard saw this as an understandable temptation, in that Jesus Christ cannot be thought of as central to Christian faith but as peripheral to the world of nature and of cosmic evolution.

If this co-extensiveness is not taken seriously, the biblical sayings about Christ and creation take on a very formal character. *With* a co-extensive view, 'St Paul's boldest sayings readily take on a literal meaning'.[4] Thus Teilhard envisages that we must:

formulate a Christology proportionate to the dimensions now attributed to the universe – that means, in recognizing that in virtue of
the mechanism of the Incarnation, Christ possesses 'universal' or
'cosmic' attributes . . . and it is precisely those attributes that make
him the personal Centre which the physics and the metaphysics of
evolution feel must exist and for which they are looking. These views
show a startling coincidence with the most fundamental Johannine
and Pauline texts and with the theology of the Greek Fathers.[5]

We see from this quotation that the Incarnation stands
at the centre of Teilhard's whole vision. But, on the basis
of co-extensiveness, its meaning is greatly enlarged. In much
traditional theological reflection the Incarnation has been
thought of as localized in one historical person and at one
point in time. But for Teilhard, 'like the Creation . . . the
Incarnation is an act co-extensive with the duration of the
world'.[6] The Incarnation is a prodigious biological operation
by which Christ is immersed in the world of matter (Incarnation), by which he assimilates and subdues it in the
depths of his own self (Cross), and by which he assumes his
function as loving, personal centre and as Christ-the-evolver
(Resurrection). It is because Christ is 'inoculated' in matter
that he can no longer be dissociated from the growth of
Spirit towards the unification, in love, of the cosmos.[7]

At first sight it is not entirely clear what role the historical
Jesus plays in Teilhard's expanded account of the Incarnation. Two points may be noted in this respect. First, God
may in some sense be said to follow the rules of the cosmic
order:

A God incarnated in history is . . . the only kind who could satisfy
the inflexible rules of a universe in which nothing is produced and
in which nothing appears except *by way of birth*.[8]

Second, and from the human standpoint, we cannot get
on to the meaning of value of the cosmic Christ, least of all
on to the fact or his concreteness, except by starting with
and only then moving out from a human Jesus who is born
and dies.

We may therefore say that Teilhard's approach to the

question about Jesus Christ is both 'from above' and 'from below'. And from both points of departure he seeks to respond as comprehensively as possible to the available evidence. 'From below' Teilhard made the fullest reference that he could, as the man he was in the epoch he was living, to the totality in which we are set at every level of its operation, not excluding its tense and tragic aspects. 'From above' he made the fullest use of that biblical and theological witness to Jesus Christ that was available to him at its own divers levels of person, community and nature.[9] Moreover, the two parallel directions of his thought, 'from above' and 'from below', which go backwards and forwards, up and down, in a restless and complex interrelationship, function in such a way that avenues of enquiry are not as easily or as readily sealed off as when only one point of departure and one direction is employed. Thus the question of the Resurrection of Christ is sealed off at an early stage in an approach 'from below' through the questions legitimately raised by a critical historical science. In Teilhard, however, the question is bound up with a total picture based on a co-extensiveness and mutual interdependence between matter and spirit.

R. R. Williams has written, with a certain humour, that for some professional German theologians 'the Pauline Epistles seem to have been written for the express purpose of providing them with relevant quotations'![10] Certainly in Teilhard's work one is impressed by the remarkable coherence at so many individual points, and in the overall picture too, between the 'scientific' and the 'Christian' ways of seeing. How far this arises through his forcing of evidence is a question which I cannot explore in this context. Suffice it to say that I believe this charge must be examined with care and not swallowed whole, since there is a very open and provisional quality about Teilhard's work which gives it a genuine resilience and flexibility in respect of changing patterns of knowledge. I suggest that this element of coherence, though not of course in any sense a firm guarantee of authenticity, should be taken seriously. For, positively, it indicates that Teilhard was making a valiant effort to remain critically faithful to the three-fold evidence which, I have suggested, must be our criterion for asking the question about Jesus Christ.

It has not been my intention in this chapter to offer a summary of Teilhard's ideas, and it is not now my intention to offer detailed criticism, since both summary and criticism are already in plentiful supply. I want to raise only one point which bears closely upon the discussion in preceding chapters.

How far is Teilhard's talk of God's action arbitrary and extrinsic in character? How far does it imply an intervention into the interconnectedness of our physical and historical life? Does he not commit us to an understanding of God's action far more literal than that of Ogden? These are delicate and complex questions. There is of course a sense in which the whole creation may, for Teilhard, be regarded as arbitrary inasmuch as it is the free act of God, though I would suspect that this attribution of arbitrariness, even in so fundamental a sense, must be treated with caution. It can be argued that for Teilhard even in the act of creation there is a certain dependence on the part of God. For Teilhard seems in some places to require that the conflict between dispersing and unifying energies which marks the whole process of cosmic evolution must be taken back into the primal step of that creative process:

It was then that the superabundant unity of life engaged, through the creation, in battle with the non-existing Multiple that was opposed to it as a contrast and a challenge.[11]

I am not sure that this kind of talk cannot be written off, as it has been by some critics, simply as early and undeveloped reflection on Teilhard's part, later to be superseded. Be this as it may, we must go on to ask whether the Incarnation (as Teilhard understands it) has an arbitrary and interventional character.

117

Teilhard appears to take the view that God has been in immanent relation, as the creative Word, with the cosmos from the outset. Teilhard holds, moreover, that the Incarnation could not occur until the evolution of the cosmos reached a point where this was appropriate:

All these preparations were cosmically, biologically, necessary if Christ was to gain a footing on the human scene.[12]

In this sense the Incarnation is no different in kind from other thresholds which have been reached and passed in the course of evolution; all contain elements both of continuity and discontinuity. Thus it may be correct to imply that the Incarnation is as natural and as supernatural, in kind but not in degree, as any other critical point in the process of creation.[13] This may be a fair representation of Teilhard's thought as long as we continue to bear in mind that the universe is never without the workings of the Word of the transcendent God, whether before or after the Incarnation. It is then a measure of the subtlety (or confusion?) of Teilhard's dialectic that we cannot draw precise lines around the roles played by the various agents in cosmogenesis. Emile Rideau, arguing (I suspect) for a stronger form of interventionism, writes that 'creation can consummate the unity that it seeks only through the intervention of a God-man'.[14] This is certainly true on Teilhard's reading of the matter. But we need to balance this with the fact that creation cannot even have the potential for the unity that it seeks except through, for example, the emergence/creation of *homo sapiens*.

For Teilhard, then, God is indeed operational in character, but always in dialectical relationship, and in luring rather than compulsive interaction, with every level of the cosmos. From this it follows that all the insights contained in the analysis of personal existence associated with Bultmann, Buri and Ogden are contained in Teilhard's pattern of thought, though they would be there set in a far richer and more comprehensive framework.

118

The loss of self-evident validity on the part of Christianity, to which I referred in Chapter 1, has lent many problematical features to the inherited doctrines concerning Jesus Christ. We now have to set those doctrines against the background of a world far older than man, of a small planet set in a vast universe among countless others, of a microcosmic world perhaps as yet hardly explored, of the human species as the product of (and participant in) an evolutionary process possibly still incomplete. This world has brought us a fuller awareness of the profound and autonomous responsibility which we bear for moral decisions affecting the whole life of man and of his environment in an era of rapid and accelerating, social, scientific and political change. It seems that we run serious risks of illusion and of dishonesty if we do not bring these and other factors into the fabric of our question about Jesus Christ. To some extent this is, of course, unavoidable. But we need to reach a fuller recognition that the structure of our question about Jesus Christ is shaped by nothing less than our whole understanding of the new, large and complex vistas which stretch out before us. At the same time, as Christians we run equally serious risks if we are unwilling to explore as strenuously as possible the witness to the person and the significance of Jesus Christ which is lodged in the broad stream of Christian tradition. However, at both these poles we meet unsolved problems, contradictions and diversity of viewpoints. At neither pole are we then vouchsafed any secure base of operation. Thus, in framing the question about Jesus Christ, we are indeed involved in a circularity of an exceedingly delicate and complex kind between what becomes authoritative for us in respect of our world and what becomes authoritative for us in respect of the tradition concerning Jesus Christ.

This has not always been thought the case. It has been thought that the authority of Jesus Christ (from the tradition) was determinative for our understanding of the world. This idea has suffered mortally from the loss of self-evident validity and from the ensuing rise of historical consciousness.

It has also been thought that the authority of the world was determinative for our understanding of Jesus Christ in the tradition. But this idea in turn must now be regarded as unacceptable in view of the surely irreversible decline of rationalistic science and the evident relativity of models. For the rules of scientific procedure of which we rely, and the scientific beliefs and valuations which we hold, are mutually determined.

At the end of the day, however, we have to affirm that, because the tradition about Jesus Christ is mediated (as much in the New Testament as anywhere else) through understandings of the world, those understandings of the world will call the tune in mobilizing, sifting and appropriating that tradition. As Buri has finely put it:

> Tradition must be understood and appropriated. Everyone who understands enacts the interpretation. What the tradition is depends upon the way in which it is understood. This power of the understanding over the tradition is at least as great as the power of the tradition over the understanding.[15]

It is therefore essential that we bring to that tradition the widest possible framework so that we do not curtail in advance the potential of that tradition over the understanding. Only thus will we be able to explore the Christian symbols which cluster around Jesus in the tradition, not only with reference to our personal existence, but also to each and every level of our reality as these are locked together in a subtle and evolutionary dialectic.

Thus the theologian who handles the theme of Jesus Christ can never expect that his subject-matter is once and for all defined, that his results are in any way assured, that his task will ever be complete. Instead, the theological enterprise concerning Jesus Christ is primarily taken up with what Troeltsch called 'the mastery of an existing situation'.[16] This means that theology is committed to the task of outlining and criticizing a 'subjective, personal interpretation and synthesis which present thinking derives from the entire situation with reference to actual living issues and for the purpose of directing future activity'.[17] So that Christian theology which belongs to the tradition about Jesus Christ 'is a living science which, far from confining us to transmitting the traditional affirmations or to engaging in apologetic', orientates us across the life of the present and participates in constructing the life of the future.[18]

Does, however, this indirect encounter with Jesus Christ give us any confidence in the ultimate worthwhileness of the theological undertaking and indeed in the worthwhileness of our lives? I have tried to suggest that we do not turn to the tradition about him in order to retreat from a godless present; nor do we turn to the world from the tradition because the latter's symbols are rootless and frothy. On the other hand, I am clear that at neither pole shall we be able to take out a comprehensive insurance against the possibility that after all the cosmic bubble will be pricked and deflated. For the negative traits which mark the theological task are never to be unmade. Nevertheless, I would suggest that if we choose to enter, at the level of our own thoughts and deeds, into the memory and expansion of Jesus' thoughts and deeds which are lodged in the complex symbolic structures of the tradition, we may uncover in them (notwithstanding their fragility) witnesses and signposts to a God of pure unbounded love who was, is, and will be working amid all the tragedy and dereliction of history to further his whole created order in that 'ascent towards the personal' by virtue of which man emerges into God's design.

That there are other witnesses and signposts is beyond dispute. Whether and in what sense Jesus has a pre-eminent place among these I feel unable to say. Nevertheless, and in no spirit of exclusiveness, I find that this personal, concrete, and therefore vulnerable witness constrains me to risk now a 'huge and *totally human* hope' that we and our world, in our present reality and in our future possibility, are dwelling and growing in nothing less than the divine milieu.

NOTES

1. Pierre Teilhard de Chardin, *Le Milieu Divin*, London 1954, paperback ed., p. 61.

2. E. E. Harris, *The Foundations of Metaphysics in Science*, London 1965, p. 32.

3. Pierre Teilhard de Chardin, *Écrits du temps de la guerre*, Paris 1965, p. 278.

4. Pierre Teilhard de Chardin, *Science and Christ*, London 1968, p.166.

5. *Op. cit.*, p. 122.

6. *Op. cit.*, p. 64. See also A. Szekeres, in: A. Szekeres (ed.), *Le Christ cosmique de Teilhard de Chardin*, Paris 1969, pp. 344-8.

7. *Op. cit.*, p. 61.

8. Pierre Teilhard de Chardin, *Le coeur de la matière*, 1950, p. 30.

9. See my article, 'Christ and Man's Place in Nature', *Theology* LXXII, 1969, pp. 98 ff.

10. R. R. Williams (ed.), *Authority and the Church*, London 1965, p. 65.

11. Pierre Teilhard de Chardin, *Writings in Time of War*, London 1968, p. 95.

12. *Science and Christ*, p. 61.

13. *The Thought of Teilhard de Chardin*, New York 1966, p. 45.

14. E. Rideau, *Teilhard de Chardin*, London 1967, p. 166.

15. F. Buri, *Theology of Existence*, p. 24.

16. E. Troeltsch, *The Social Teaching*, p. 1003.

17. E. Troeltsch, *The American Journal of Theology* XVII, 1913, pp. 12 f.

18. E. Vermeil, *La Pensée religieuse de Troeltsch*, Strasbourg and Paris 1922, p. 4.

Conclusion

At the end of Chapter I, I promised the conclusion that any attempts which we might make to frame an answer to the question about Jesus Christ would be fragmentary, inconclusive and paradoxical in character. This has proved to be the case. Teilhard's contribution extends the field of our vision but itself bristles with unresolved problems.

Now this untidiness is not simply due to the problem of historical evidence. It arises in the main because the question about Jesus Christ always impels us towards further questions about God and the world – questions so comprehensive and mysterious as to induce mental and spiritual vertigo. We are then confronted by the particular problem (which is crucial to christology) how, if at all, we may understand God as *operational*, as involved in *deeds*. I would follow Ogden and Teilhard, in their very different ways, and say that we can only approach this problem by examining the fragmentary, inconclusive, and paradoxical operations which we undertake in ourselves, in community and in our worldly environment.

Thus our handling of the question about Jesus Christ cannot be separated from the continually changing understanding which we have of ourselves and of the world – an understanding which derives not so much from passive inspection as from the experience of, and reflection upon, these deeds. There is therefore an ineradicable element of mysticism, though a mysicism of action, about our search for the identity of Jesus Christ. The often quoted conclusion of Albert Schweitzer's *The Quest of the Historical Jesus* indicates vividly the place where, above all, the question about Jesus Christ is to be asked:

'He comes to us as One unknown, without a name, as of old, by the lake-side, He came to those men who knew Him not. He speaks to us the same word: "Follow thou me!" and sets us to the tasks which He has to fulfil for our time. He commands. And to those who obey Him, whether they be wise or simple, He will reveal Himself in the toils, the conflicts, the sufferings which they shall pass through in His fellowship, and, as an ineffable mystery, they shall learn in their own experience Who He Is.'

For Further Reading

S. Cave, *The Doctrine of the Person of Christ* (London: Duckworth, 1952).

J. B. Cobb, 'The Finality of Christ in a Whiteheadian Perspective', in *The Finality of Christ*, (ed.) Dow Kirkpatrick (New York: Abingdon Press, 1966).

J. M. Creed, *The Divinity of Jesus Christ* (London: Collins Fontana, 1964).

F. G. Downing, *The Church and Jesus* (London: SCM Press and Naperville, Ill: Allenson, 1968).

A. D. Galloway, *The Cosmic Christ* (London: James Nisbet and New York: Harper and Row, 1951).

Van A. Harvey, *The Historian and the Believer* (London: SCM Press and New York: Macmillan, 1967).

E. G. Jay, *Son of Man, Son of God* (London: SPCK, 1965).

J. N. D. Kelly, *Early Christian Doctrines* (London: A & C Black, 1958), chs. 6, 11, 12.

J. Knox, *The Humanity and Divinity of Christ* (Cambridge: Cambridge University Press, 1969).

F. Loofs, *What is the Truth about Jesus Christ*? (Edinburgh: T & T Clark and New York: Charles Scribner's Sons, 1913).

W. R. Matthews, *The Problem of Christ in the Twentieth Century* (London and New York: Oxford University Press, 1950).

C. F. Mooney, *Teilhard de Chardin and the Mystery of Christ* (London: Collins and New York: Harper and Row, 1966).

W. Pannenberg, *Jesus – God and Man* (London: SCM Press and Philadelphia: Westminster Press, 1968).

W. N. Pittenger (ed.), *Christ for Us Today* (London: SCM Press, 1968).

H. Rashdall, *Jesus, Human and Divine* (London and New York: Andrew Melrose, 1922).

Index

Proper names, etc. in the notes to each chapter are not included in this index

Authority, 16 f., 41, 119

Barr, James, 22 ff.
Barth, Karl, 44
Bible, 12, 16, 23, 25, 79 ff.
Braaten, Carl, 21
Bonhoeffer, Dietrich, 26
Bultmann, Rudolf, 43, 46 ff., 63 ff., 71, 76, 78, 91, 101
Buri, Fritz, 63 ff., 74, 78, 81, 94 ff., 120

Cipher, 77 f., 82 ff., 120
Co-extensiveness, 114 f.
Cosmic Christ, 113 f.

Development, 33 f.
Dibelius, Martin, 46 f.
Dilthey, Wilhelm, 32
Dogmatics, 36 ff.
Downing, Gerald, 22 ff.
Dualism, 59 f.

Ebeling, Gerhard, 24, 48, 71
Eschatological event, 53 f., 56, 94 f.
Evolution, 114 f.
Existence, 84 f., 100, 108
  authentic 52 ff., 67 ff.

Faith, 97 f.
Form criticism, 46 ff.

Fuchs, Ernst, 71

Gardiner, Patrick, 42
God, action of, 49 f., 54, 56, 65 ff., 117 f.

Harnack, A. von, 19
Harvey, Van A., 74, 107
Heidegger, 49, 51 f., 53, 61, 65, 76 f.
Historical criticism, 16, 24 ff., 29 ff.
Holy Spirit, 17

Incarnation, 115 f., 118
Individuality, 31 ff.

Jaspers, Karl, 74, 76 ff., 96 f., 100, 109 f.
Jesus Christ
  character of, 48, 72 f.
  uniqueness of, 14 f., 55 ff., 61, 63 ff., 70 f., 78, 83, 89 ff., 104, 107, 114
  – and history, 13, 46 ff., 63 ff., 115

Käsemann, Ernst, 71
Kierkegaard, Soren, 82 f.
Knowledge, 97 f.
  'iron-curtain view of', 107 ff.
Knox, John, 47

McIntyre, John, 22 ff.
Maurice, F. D., 73
Metaphysics, 85 f.
Myth, 49, 55 f., 63 ff., 76

New Testament, 15, 35, 65, 67 f.,
    89, 96, 100, 103 f., 120
Nicene Creed, 9 f., 12, 73
Nietzsche, Frederick, 82 f.

Ogden, Schubert M., 63, 65 ff.,
    91, 107, 112, 117, 123

Philosophy of history, 42 f.
Probability, 42 f., 58
Process philosophy, 66, 73

Relativism, 19 f.
Revelation, 21 ff., 78 f.
Rideau, Emile, 118

Ritschl, Albrecht, 103
Robinson, James M., 43, 71

Salvation history, 40 f.
Schleiermacher, Friedrich, 31, 103
Schweitzer, Albert, 94 f., 103,
    123 f.
Secularization, 30
Sykes, Norman, 43
Symbol, 74, 99, 104 ff.

Teilhard de Chardin, Pierre,
    112 ff., 123
Tennant, F. R., 31
Tradition, 12 f., 16, 18, 27, 119
Transcendence, 85 ff., 100, 103
Troeltsch, Ernst, 16, 24, 29 ff., 48,
    52, 54, 57 f., 71, 109, 112 f.

Werner, Martin, 94ff., 103